THE SALES YOGI

The Yogis, abandoning attachment,
act with body, mind, intelligence
and even with the senses,
only for the purpose of purification.

The Bhagwad Gita
Chapter 5. Verse 11.

THE SALES YOGI

MASTER THE CRAFT OF SELLING IN THE MODERN WORLD THROUGH THE WISDOM OF THE YOGIS

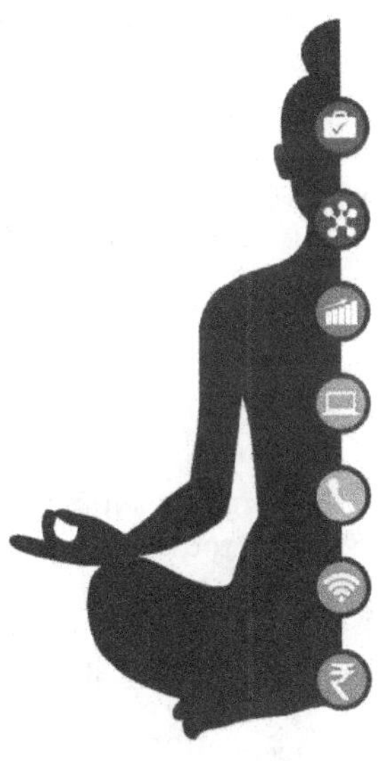

By

SANJEEVV K SOMANATH

Bonus Chapters By:

JENIL DHOLAKIA

MUGDHA PRADHAN

THE SALES YOGI

Published by Happy Self Publishing
www.happyselfpublishing.com

PREFACE

We are all salespersons. Sounds preposterous? Picture yourself in a car going for a long drive with your friends. Goa, did you say? Good beginning. You ask for that 'aux cable' or Bluetooth pairing and play your favourite tracks. Are you just sharing your songs or are you selling the notion that you have a good taste in music? Talk about technocrats.

An engineer has to 'sell' the bridge that he is envisioning to his team before actually building it. A musician has to 'sell' his composition to the music producer to make it see the light of the day. A writer has to 'sell' his story. Heck, even a lover has to 'sell' emotions to woo the heart of his/her beloved.

Parents 'sell' values to their children through fables and teachings so that they can imbibe them in the future. We 'sell' the concept of God for a saner world around us. The government 'sells' the fear of punishment to maintain law and order. If you are still here, congratulations, you have just realized the fact that you are a salesperson, your occupation notwithstanding.

Despite constantly selling something all our lives, we have been brought up in a way that the words 'selling' and 'money' are deemed immoral. This is precisely the reason why every good salesman, well I am talking about the people who are into sales professionally, is a good salesman when he or she doesn't 'sell' stuff on the face.

For instance, picture yourself waiting for a friend outside a mall, and your mobile's battery is draining. You look around, constantly checking the time. A salesman approaches, offering you books at unbelievable prices. After a while, another salesman stands next to you. He isn't approaching you and you sigh in relief for not doing so. From the corner of your eyes, you notice that he is reading a book silently and smiling while turning the pages. Curious, you approach him and ask if it's a book worth spending time and money on. No price for guessing whom you'd buy the book from.

What the other salesman did was selling experience instead of selling the product. He understood the fact that 'selling' is a dirty word so the subtle approach works in his favour. There is an insight here. The salesman knows that you might have ample time to kill. A book or magazine is available right inside the mall, but how would you know which book or magazine to buy? Simple, by watching someone enjoy reading something. Sell the sizzle, not just the steak, states the ancient wisdom.

While we are at it, let me dwell some more on the sizzle part. There was a coffee shop right next to the metro station. No matter how much the coffee shop folks tried to promote themselves, the commuters just won't abandon the metro station to have a cuppa. The coffee shop hired an intelligent advertising agency. They placed billboards at the metro station, lo and behold, the coffee shop was abuzz with commuters.

Guess what image the billboards carry? Of people yawning. Yup, yawning. The insight at work here is: Yawning is contagious. 70% of people yawn when they see someone else yawning. Want to try? Stop here right now. Google a yawning pic and come back. I am sure you'll find yourself stifling a yawn or two just by the mere thought of it.

The insight had to work. People yawned looking at the 'contagious billboard', which was armed with motion sensors that sensed people yawning and made the video in the billboard yawn, creating an epidemic of sorts at the metro station. The line revealed: Luckily, we have the cure, followed by young women serving coffee. Strike when the iron is hot, proclaims the ancient wisdom.

These two instances, despite being different kinds, with one being imaginary and the other a true incident, one being 'cost-effective' while the other being 'tech-savvy', still bear the similarity of being connected to ancient wisdom, revisited with a new perspective.

That's 'The Sales Yogi' by Sanjeevv K. Somanath for you.

Inspired by the ancient wisdom of Bhagwad Geeta and Seven Chakras, 'The Sales Yogi' offers you new-age insights that can help you go a long way in life.

The beauty of reading and revisiting ancient scriptures like the Bhagwad Geeta is that they have something new to offer every time you take the pains of reading it. Unfortunately, we place such scriptures on such a high pedestal and worship them that we seldom invest time to read and understand them.

The same holds true for 'The Sales Yogi'. It's a book that has to be read and reread round the year, not as a handbook of sales, but as a friend, philosopher, and guide. Recommending this book to friends and relatives would imply that you truly care for them and wish to see them doing well in life.

We all have been blessed with skills that we keep honing all through our lives, but in this process of honing skills, we often forget to work on our internal mechanism or simply put, to look within ourselves.

'The Sales Yogi' makes no claims of changing your life. If books could change lives, the world would have been a much better place. What it will change is – Your perspective of looking at your professional life or perhaps personal life too. Sanjeevv K. Somanath pens this book in a way that finds resonance within the recesses of every heart.

After all, deep down inside, we all are selling something. So, why not sell better and become Sales Yogis? Time to turn the proverbial page and begin a new chapter. Bon voyage!

Prakash Gowda - Author of Baker's Dozen and Ghalib Unplugged, Writer, Director, and Ad-man.

TABLE OF CONTENT

SOME PRAISE FOR THE BOOK

I really love the intention and the deep thought process behind this book. Most salespeople are often just chasing numbers, which is not entirely a bad thing to do, but in the chase, they end up forgetting why it is that they are doing what they do. I honestly think sales is one of the most important roles an organization can have. Even right now, as the CEO of ThriveFNC, I personally spend nearly 30-50% of my time every day in sales and there's a reason why I do it. Every sale we make or every lead that doesn't convert teaches us invaluable lessons about the work we do. If someone's buying what we are selling, then it's a confirmation that the services we offer are of value to another being. The day I stop being of value, is the day I cease to exist and therefore I look at sales as one of my holy grails when it comes to running a business. That being said, most salespeople don't understand how multidimensional the sales process is in itself. I think this book brings the right kind of focus using the Bhagwad Gita as a guiding light. I am personally impressed by the aspects of sales you are covering in this book Sanjeev and I look forward to a whole new approach towards sales from the readers of this book. May your tribe increase!

Mugdha Pradhan - Functional Nutritionist and the Founder of Thrive FNC

This indeed is a very interesting take on a topic that's so commonly written about. Juxtaposing the seven chakras with the attributes of a salesperson is a very daring & insightful approach. Chakras are powerful energy centers present in each one of us & they represent a particular emotion/quality, which is very well covered in this book and made it relevant to those who are in the client servicing profile. Sales is a very competitive field & one needs to be in their best game, not just physically, but even emotionally, mentally & intellectually. This becomes a blueprint for anyone who wishes to excel not just at their work, but also in their personal life & create a holistic work-life balance. It's time we apply Indian wisdom to the mainstream world, where it really matters the most. By breaking down ancient concepts into simple & relevant manners, the book allows one to see the same things from a different perspective. To those who seek with an open heart & mind, shall find answers within the pages of this book.

Jenil Dholakia - Yogini and Founder of Jenil Dholakia Yoga

THE STORY OF THE SALES YOGI

A couple of years ago I quit my job. I quit because I was no longer feeling the passion. I quit because I felt lost. I quit because I was burnt out and started to drop my performance. I wondered why I felt the lack of connection to something that had given me so much joy and success.

As I sought answers I decided to turn within and understand what is it that kept me from being at my peak. As a salesperson, I knew the role itself had its ups and downs. But this was different. It was more internal than external. I invested my time in self-development and cracking the code to sustain my passion for the work I love doing sales.

I had the privilege of meeting some amazing mentors, interacting with some great sales minds globally, and also learning a great deal about emotions, attitude, and happiness, and finding a correlation between them and sales performance to create a learning experience for sales professionals and small business owners.

My research led me to the Bhagwad Gita and that opened my eyes to the absolute knowledge the book carries. The next few months gave more structure and insights that blew my mind. It was all there always. Simple yet so deep. Teachings that reinforced what I always knew but never grasped the importance of it. My mind was on a high as I started to create the Seven Chakras of Sales Program and most importantly my book - The Sales Yogi.

With the encouragement and support of my family, some friends, and a few amazing communities I became a part of, I started to make great progress in my research and writing. Today I stand having completed my book and onto its publication. The first batch of The Sales Yogi has already been launched and am impacting lives as I write this.

I think the journey of ups and downs is a story of every person in the profession of Sales. It is essentially a people's profession and that makes it a profession that demands great self-awareness. It is unjust to keep all sales coaching and training focused on skills only. The key aspects of emotions and attitudes are often overlooked or given lesser importance. It is time to change this. By combining teachings from the Bhagwad Gita into the cut-throat sales profession, I aim to disrupt sales training as we know it. My mission is to help professionals and business owners avoid the pitfalls I had in my journey by converting my mess into this message of The Sales Yogi. Come. Join me on this epic journey of going within. Let's create an army of Yogis in sales.

Sanjeevv k Somanath

DEDICATIONS

MY BELOVED FATHER

From the first time I witnessed work, I saw my father - Somanath Balakrishna, epitomized the Karma Yogi. His work ethics and commitment shone through his work and that gained him immense respect amongst his peers and clients. Our home had his office in it back in the day and a majority of our time went into witnessing his outlook towards his work. The ease with which he went through his day at work and then totally switched off to enjoy his time with his family and doing the things that he loved was amazing.

As I started my career his only golden advice to me was to be dutiful to what has been entrusted to me as my work. It took me some years to fully understand the essence of what he said. I have grown to witness many terms like mindfulness, surrender, focus, a service mindset, and many more; only to realize my father embodied all of these.

This book is a dedication to him and his work. He inspired us to do better and truly be in a state of flow when working.

I love you, Dad. You are missed but we see you in us. I only wish you were here to physically witness this book though I know you are seeing me from up above. I feel your presence with me always. Guiding me. For all the wonderful lessons you have taught me and my sisters, I bow down in gratitude.

MY LOVELY MOTHER

It is not an exaggeration when we say mothers are Goddesses on the face of the earth. They are life bearers. Made to be a reflection of the almighty on us. This is so true for who you are my lovely mother - Kalpagam. Like your name, for me, you are the name of the Goddess here in my world. From the time I have gained the sense to understand things, one thing has been clear - you are the most loving and patient soul.

There is an ocean of goodness in you, and it has never gone dry. I look up to you Mom and wish I had half of the patience and gratitude you carry. We look for inspiration outside but with you in my life, I have had no reason to look elsewhere. You have picked me up when I was down. You have been the undying support for me and my dreams. You have guided me and held me through the toughest phases of my life.

Many aspects of this book resonate with me because I have an example to show what devotional service is. You are Bhakti. You are Shakti. You are my mother, my life. I love you from the bottom of my heart and dedicate this book to you. Bless me like you always have.

MY FRIEND, MY BROTHER

My dear friend, Chetan. I finally got down to writing a book as we spoke about so many times. You were an elder brother to me in all the truest emotions of it. The passion and energy you carried in your work have always been inspirational. I am sure many who are reading this book and have worked with you as I have, will agree to this. You epitomized love for work. Your success and fame were results of that love and I am lucky to witness that. I miss you dearly and would have loved to read this book to you. Your love motivates me to go farther and faster. For all your wisdom and guidance you gave me, I bow down in gratitude my friend. My many hours of talking and sharing with you have given me the clarity to write this book. It is a dedication to who you were and who you inspired us to become.

धृतराष्ट्र उवाच
धर्मक्षेत्रे कुरुक्षेत्रे समवेता युयुत्सवः।
मामकाः पाण्डवाश्चैव किमकुर्वत सञ्जय।

Dhritarashtra said: O Sanjaya, after my sons and
the sons of Pandu assembled in the place of
pilgrimage at Kurukshetra, what did they do?

Chapter 1. Verse 1.

The Bhagwad Gita

INTRODUCTION

Seeing the prospects assembled in the system, the boss turns to the sales team and asks, "Tell me, which prospect among these is your closure?"

The "boss" is *Dhritarashtra*. Blind to what is happening on the field. But the king nonetheless. The king needs to know if the war has been won. He need not get on the battlefield himself. He can take the help of information. Information that systems and procedures give him.

That "system" is *Sanjaya*. The one with the divine vision to see what is happening on the field. An ability enabled by the actions of the warriors. The Sales Warriors!

Like the armies gathered in great numbers on the battlefield of Kurukshetra, armies of Sales professionals gather in great numbers. Sometimes in competition with others. Sometimes in competition with themselves. Sometimes in competition with skills. Sometimes in competition with emotions.

Aspiring to be victorious.

Like *Arjuna* in the *Mahabharata*. The supreme archer and the great warrior.

The sales superstars gobble every target ever thrown at them.

They keep moving. Hustling. Conquering clients under the arrows of their charm.

Till they reach a point where they go numb. Seeing greater challenges in front of them. Challenges that test their skills. Challenges that test their knowledge. Challenges that shake the very foundation of their image and beliefs.

Exasperated, they turn to for help. To be able to overcome the frigidity that has come upon them. Seeking to go deeper within and with-out. Choosing to know the secret to everlasting euphoria in the acquisition of a client.

That is the secret I seek to deliver in this book for you.

This book is not a spiritual download of what the *Bhagwad Gita* teaches. It will take many more years to be able to fully understand the amazing spiritual wealth the *Bhagwad Gita* carries.

This book is a very honest and humble attempt to seek how the teachings and stories within the *Bhagwad Gita* can be interpreted in the light of Sales.

Like a warrior, whose aim is to win wars, a Salesperson is expected to seal deals. One after the other. Skill is one aspect of the Sales 'persona' and also the most worked on. However, that in itself is not enough. Successful salespeople give importance to what is within them. The internal mechanism, like a Yogi. Shining inside out.

In the Bhagwad Gita, Lord Krishna tells Arjuna –

दुःखेष्वनुद्विग्रमनाः सुखेषु विगतस्पृहः।
वीतरागभयक्रोधः स्थितधीर्मुनिरुच्यते।

One who is not disturbed in mind even amidst the threefold miseries or elated when there is happiness, and who is free from attachment, fear, and anger, is a sage of steady mind.

Chapter 2. Verse 56.

This is the path of the Yogi.

When you look at this in the light of Sales, you realize how our obsession with the emotions of despair and elation, tied to the results of the efforts we put in to close a deal, often does more damage to us than good.

In the chapters of this book, I have tried to cover some useful meta concepts in the most practical ways to imbibe for each of you to emerge a true Yogi. A Sales Yogi.

If you have this book in your hand currently, I am assuming you are a sales warrior or you know someone who is one.

My wish for you is that you take the concepts and tips presented here, apply them in your sales life, and shine through stronger than ever!

Happy Selling, Yogis!

PART I:

THE FIRST STEP

या निशा सर्वभूतानां तस्यां जागर्ति संयमी।
यस्यां जाग्रति भूतानि सा निशा पश्यतो मुनेः

That which is the night to all beings, in that the self-controlled man is awake; when all beings are awake, that is the night for the Muni (sage) who sees.

Chapter 2. Verse 69.

Priya and Umar are colleagues. Both are good performers but there is something that Priya does that takes her over the targets set every quarter. Everyone thinks both are equally skilled and passionate about what they do. The secret to Priya's success just baffles everyone.

Finally, Umar decides to ask Priya about her secret sauce.

Priya being the great team player spills her greatest secret. She tells Umar her day starts early at five AM every day. Before the sun rises, she is up. She spends the first hour with herself. Having a cup of coffee, meditating, exercising, and so on. She devotes five minutes every day to visualizing her day at work - making notes and planning her day. In this way the moment her workday starts, she is ready. She knows exactly where she needs to focus and what her day looks like.

That, she says, is the only thing she does differently from Umar.

The Bhagwad Gita mentions two types of people in one of its chapters.

There are two classes of intelligent people, it says.

One is intelligent and absorbed in the gratification of what we call "material" pursuits.

The other one knows the power within, is introspective, and awake to self-realization.

Like the energy junctions that we call *Nadis* in Yoga which represent the chakras, I want you to strive to be in the second category of people through the energy junctions of sales - the seven chakras. These are aspects that are intrinsically important and their impact on how you approach your sales life is immense. Embrace the wisdom that is a part of one of the oldest texts in the world - The Bhagwad Gita as presented through this book. Starting with a habit that you need to absolutely form - waking up early in the morning! This is one non-negotiable habit you have to cultivate. If you have brought this book because you want to transform how you approach sales, this is the first task for you.

In the verse at the beginning of this chapter, the Gita delves into this subject meta-physically, but to understand it in light of this book, let's focus on the aspect of night and day. The importance of waking in the *"Brahmamuhurta."* The morning is an opportunity for a fresh start every day. Part of the reason and the motivation of so many of us globally waking up well before the sunrise and getting to work on us. Some take to meditation, while some partake to exercise. But we all understand the importance of being in the club of early risers.

It is important to understand that when we spend the time introspecting and working within, we are preparing ourselves up for anything the external world can throw at us.

The modern-day salesperson is bombarded with accessibility tools. As the line between the day and the night thins, what you decided for yourself today will matter most. In the further chapters, we look into the most important aspects of transforming yourself into a Sales Yogi. These are skills that are time tested and known to be important for you to succeed in sales.

But what I will try to do is to give you a perspective on these in light of what is written in the books of all ages - The Bhagwad Gita.

The first step to understanding these is to WAKE UP!

From the slumber of what you know to the light of new knowledge - early in the morning when the ignorant sleep.

Remember, when you control your mind and yourself, you become a friend to yourself. Read it again. Slowly.

Think of what you think you can achieve by committing to waking up every day an hour before the sun rises. Think of it in terms of your mental, emotional, and physical aspects. Connect it back to your duty as a salesperson. How it will affect your workday. This will be a tricky thing to do. Try to be as specific as possible to your work. Avoid generic statements on the benefits of waking up early, meditation, or exercise.

REFLECTION TIME #1:

Once you have thought about it, write this down in the below section or print it and keep it on your desk. This is your purpose statement. The answer to the question of why to invest your time into this transformational journey and do what is prescribed in the book and beyond.

____

____

____

____

____

____

____

The reason that I am stressing this is that many of the things presented in this book will need you to reflect and think. What better time is there in the day to do that than early in the morning!

When you wake up and commit to yourself to give that first hour of the day to yourself, you will realize the wonder that is self-realization. The Bhagwad

Gita says there is no person more knowledgeable than the self-realized one. In further chapters, you will come across some metaphysical concepts and some practices. Both are important for you to understand so you can invoke and master the seven chakras of sales -

1. Attitude.
2. Creativity and Emotions.
3. Passion, Persistence, and Knowledge.
4. Client-Centric Mindset.
5. Communication and Expression.
6. Intuition and Openness.
7. Network and Influence.

So, let's jump straight into the depth of the energies and look at our foundation - Attitude. Too much talent has gone to waste because of this aspect - which is the Mooladhara or the Root Chakra.

THE SEVEN CHAKRAS OF SALES

सर्वाणीन्द्रियकर्माणि प्राणकर्माणि चापरे।
आत्मसंयमयोगाग्नौ जुह्वति ज्ञानदीपिते।

Some sacrifice all the functions of the senses and those of the breath (vital energy or Prana) in the fire of the Yoga of self-restraint kindled by knowledge.

Chapter 4. Verse 27

The Bhagwad Gita

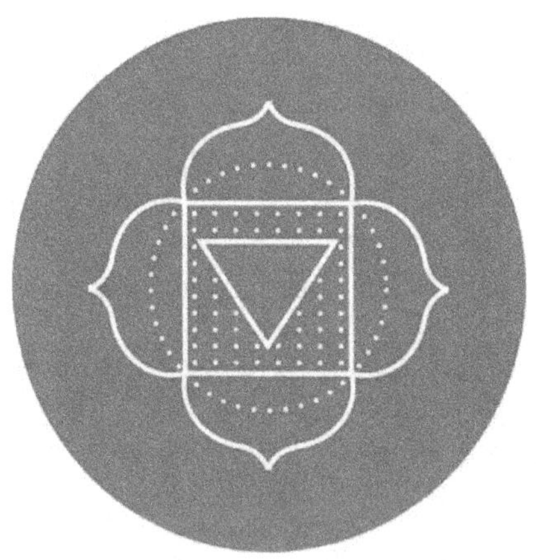

THE MOOLADHARA / ROOT CHAKRA OF ATTITUDE

कर्मण्येवाधिकारस्ते मा फलेषु कदाचन।
मा कर्मफलहेतुर्भूर्मा ते सङ्गोऽस्त्वकर्मणि

Thy right is to work only, but never with its fruits;
let not the fruits of action be thy motive, nor let
thy attachment be to inaction.

Chapter 2. Verse 47.

The quarter has not been good for the entire company. The sales team is under pressure. All seem to be crumbling below it too. Faced with the challenge of turning around sales amidst the pandemic, Ravi sets out to reskill, relearn, and pivot his selling style. He understands that his focus should be on what he can control - his actions.

Rahul on the other hand like much of the sales team is struggling with the momentum. He and his cronies are busy discussing how they will not be able to meet the targets for the next six months. A month passes by and they reach review time again. The entire sales team except Ravi is without closures and a dry pipeline. Ravi presents his data and he has closed two accounts and his pipeline looks great for the next six months. How did he do it?

Rahul and his cronies are asked to follow Ravi's approach to work. His approach is simple - to focus on what he needs to do to get to his goal and not the goal itself. A simple difference in attitude - the foundation on which careers and success are built.

The root chakra or the Mooladhara is your foundation.

For every salesperson to ever have walked this Earth this quality has been a difference-maker. Attitude.

Attitude can decide your fate and how far you go on the journey of being a great salesperson. No wonder that it is the first Chakra we need to invoke. Its element the Earth depicts groundedness and being a channel for survival for everything living on this planet.

What is the right attitude to have for the salesperson? A lot has been said and heard in this regard. In my experience *surrendering and being dutiful* is the right attitude. This may seem a bit out of line with the conventional thought process but the objective of the book is not to repeat what we already know. The objective is to base our transformation through Yogic principles in the Bhagwad Gita.

Let us come back to surrender and duty. To understand this, let's break the verse at the beginning of this section down.

Your right, for whatever it is that you do in your life, is with the work. Your right is not on its results or fruits, as is mentioned in the verse. Yet you are supposed to keep doing your duty and not make inaction your friend.

Quite a bit for a salesperson maybe? It is not. Like it was not for Arjuna when he got obsessed with the results of his pulling the string of his bow and shooting the arrow. Seeing his family, teacher and brothers lined up in arms before him, Arjuna froze.

He was unable to move his limbs to fight. His mouth dried up. His whole body trembled, the hair stood on the back of his neck and his greatest weapon, his bow, was slipping from his hand.

Fast forward to the current time.

Many times, you find yourselves frozen in the sales pipeline.

Be it at any stage. Starting from prospecting to the final YES for the closure. You believe you have put out your greatest weapons and still, nothing moves. The deal (your bow) seems to be slipping from your hands. That feeling freezes you. Like Arjuna. The army of prospect is in front of you. But you are having one or maybe two to focus on.

Ask any of the greatest salespeople and they will tell you the secret to a great sales record is being disciplined. Being dutiful.

In the Bhagwad Gita, Lord Krishna tells Arjuna –

स्वधर्ममपि चावेक्ष्य न विकम्पितुमर्हसि।
0धर्म्याद्धि युद्धाच्छ्रेयोऽन्यत्क्षत्रियस्य न विद्यते।

Further, having regard to thy duty, shouldn't not waver, for there is nothing higher for a Kshatriya than a righteous war.

Chapter 2. Verse 31.

It is the understanding that prescribed tasks affect your duties, which will form the first part of what makes a Sales Yogi.

Like Arjuna is reminded that his duty to fight for *Dharma* is the only thing that matters, your duty as a salesperson is to SELL, and proudly.

This may seem to be a very broad statement. Let's do a simple exercise to uncover what these duties could mean for you, with regards to what you sell. Answer the below question. This time think beyond just your targets and numbers. Think of the larger vision you are a part of. Either your own or your employer's. Be as descriptive as possible. That will help you break your response down further and see what you need to start focusing on as a salesperson above the daily grind.

REFLECTION TIME #2: Answer the below question.

What is your duty as a Salesperson?

____

____

____

____

____

The call of duty has been considered a great motivation for action forever. The Bhagwad Gita, a dialogue on the battlefield of Kurukshetra speaks about it. But it is also a part of every military organization in the current times too. Duty reigns supreme. The mindset of being dutiful drives the person to many great lengths in a battle. Sometimes even to the brink of being superhuman.

Now as a salesperson, you may not need to be a superhuman. You need to be true to your duty. Go through the process of prospecting, qualifying, reaching out, pitching, submitting a proposal, and finally getting to the closure with utmost discipline.

Your reputation depends on creating this mindset.

अथ चैत्त्वमिमं धर्म्यं संग्रामं न करिष्यसि।
ततः स्वधर्मं कीर्तिं च हित्वा पापमवाप्स्यसि।

If, however, you do not perform your religious duty of fighting, then you will certainly incur sins for neglecting your duties and thus lose your reputation as a fighter.

Chapter 2. Verse 33.

The great warrior Arjuna, bestowed with special weapons for his immense skill and grit, was on the verge of abandoning the battlefield. Overcome by the stress of managing his emotions. In this thought, he was choosing to neglect his specific duty as a *Kshatriya,* and that would mean he was losing all his fame and incurring a sin that would lead him straight to hell.

In the sales world, neglecting duties can bear the same heavy price.

You have written down your specific duties as a salesperson. If you are not completely focused on the duties, you will stand to lose more than gain. There is no substitute for being dutiful. **There are no shortcuts.**

If you have done the exercise mentioned above already you will have a fair sense of how the attitude of being dutiful is going to be the change that will make your life in sales easier.

If you have not done the exercise, I ask you to do it before you read further as you need to introspect and come up with what you feel are your true duties as a salesperson.

This is important to know as that will set you up to be on the path of the *Karma Yogi.*

The Karma Yogi in Sales

So, who exactly is a Karma Yogi?

As you would have guessed by now the Karma Yogi is one who is committed to the task, his duty. But there is a metaphysical law to making this work for you faster and better. In one of the most powerful programs I had been a part of, I came across this concept of the fourth level of manifestation in which you see yourself as a channel for the universe. Specific to a task. In our case, the task of selling.

The reason I am referring to this is to understand who truly is a Karma Yogi. What do the Yogi think? Where does the Yogi base his or her motivation? How does the Yogi achieve things without being attached to the fruits of the action?

To find the answer to these questions, let us go back to a verse in the Bhagwad Gita.

कर्मण्यकर्म यः पश्येदकर्मणि च कर्म यः।
स बुद्धिमान् मनुष्येषु स युक्तः कृत्स्नकर्मकृत्।

He who seeth inaction in action and action in inaction, he is wise among men; he is a Yogi and performer of all actions.

Chapter 4. Verse 18.

Action in Inaction and Inaction in Action. Sounds like an oxymoron, doesn't it? Let's look at what the idea entails.

Action as we commonly understand means movement. Movement of the body. Movement of the hands and feet. A movement to do what is needed. A movement to sell. We are the *doer* here. The one who does what is needed to sell products and services to our customers. It is this very idea that we are the doer that binds us back to results.

When the idea that one is only a doer vanishes, even action is no action at all.

It will not bind one to the fruititive benefits. Let me go deeper into this concept. If you identify yourself with the actionless self, be an *Akarta (the non-doer)*, no matter what work or how much of it is done, the action is no action at all. This is the concept of inaction in action. A quick thought to how you do not feel tired doing the things that you truly surrender to and go with the flow will help you see what being inactive in action is. By such a practice and mindset, action loses its binding nature as what drives you is not the outcomes of what you do, but the love for what you do. This of course needs a lot of work and attention and is very well covered in the Seven Chakras of Sales Program that I run.

Let's now explore the other side of this coin. If one thinks that he or she is the doer, he/she is in effect always in action. Even in silence and physical inaction, they are in action. The restless mind will never cease to be in action and actions of the mind are as real as real actions. Hence, we are always in action for the mind is mostly at work. This is the concept of Action in Inaction. The modern-day concept of workaholism. Look around and you will be reminded we have been told many times to be able to switch off from work while at work. Maybe you advised this to someone you know too. The inability to give the mind the rest signifies an action in inaction. We think. We brood. We are in a trance thinking about work and how we have to "do" things. The pressure keeps mounting and very soon it catches up to us and makes our lives miserable.

Having understood both Action in Inaction and Inaction in Action, read the above verse again.

The one who understands that he or she can be active when inactive and inactive when active becomes a Yogi and when he or she brings this mindset to work, the *Karya* and the *Karma*, he or she becomes a *Karma Yogi*. Let me help you understand this mindset further.

Picture yourself driving a speedboat that is cruising along the river. The speedboat is in action. You are still and witnessing it moving ahead cutting through the waves. You are being inactive in activity yet moving ahead. As the speedboat moves ahead the trees along the shore seem to be moving in the opposite direction. We all know trees don't move. Yet they seem to be active. That is Action in Inaction.

In the above example when you understand that though you seem to be doing the task of driving the boat, the only thing, in essence, you are doing is playing the throttle to your needs. You are not driving the speedboat. The mechanism is. The gears are. Yet you are active as you are now the *channel* to drive the speedboat ahead. Thereby being inactive in action. As this happens the trees on the shores though inanimate seems to be moving in the opposite direction. Thereby being active inaction.

For the salesperson, this means you are the captain of the speedboat that has mechanisms in it - what we know as processes, product, marketing, and others. Your duty as a salesman is to drive this machine to reach a destination. In doing so, your mind like the true monkey will try to be a master. But a true Yogi understands this and knows the restless mind will never allow for us to be truly inactive. Hence, he/she undertakes activities to tame the monkey.

What is needed is for one to understand and imbibe that one is not "doing" something because he or she is supposed to do it but because he or she is meant to be doing it.

When you believe truly that your purpose is to do your duty well and see both action and inaction as being a part of what you do and how you sell, you will see your attitude shift. The feeling of opening yourself to your company and being a channel for the growth of it will propel yourself to a higher pedestal than people who do not understand the true essence of why we are being told repeatedly to be committed and focused on the purpose.

The mooladhara or the root chakra of Attitude is thus invoked.

REFLECTION TIME #3:

Look back into your work and see if there were situations where you put your head down and did what was needed to do. Not approaching it as a task but just being in a flow and you achieved what you set out to do with lesser burnout. Write down that event in the below section.

____

____

____

____

____

____

____

Keep it handy with you. It will be a reminder of how you think being a Karma Yogi helped you unknowingly. When you know this, you can now consciously work to get better at this root chakra - the attitude of a Karma Yogi! As the Root Chakra in Yoga helps maintain a sense of groundedness and inner stability, the Karma Yogi attitude will ensure you remain still even in the most pressing and challenging situations as a salesperson.

At the beginning of the section, I spoke about the importance of waking up an hour before the sun rises. Pick that time of the day to start your workday with the below affirmation. I have six more affirmations further in the book that will help you make the mindset shift needed to start transforming yourself in your sales career. In the bonus chapter of the book, we will know more about a few meditative and yoga techniques that will help imbibe these affirmations further.

BONUS#1
The Sales Yogi Mooladhara Affirmation Statement:

I am grounded and I know I am a channel. I do not do things; I make things happen AS me.

Summarizing the traits that make up for the Attitude or the Mooladhara Chakra of a Sales Yogi:

- The Sales Yogi is dutiful.
- The Sales Yogi understands that he/she is meant to sell and focuses on the larger vision at hand.
- The Sales Yogi knows how action and inaction are all part of the duty and sets his/her attention to mastering these and being a true *Karma Yogi*.
- The Sales Yogi is attached to action and not the fruits of the action.
- The Sales Yogi is humble and grounded.
- The Sales Yogi embraces his/her role in the organization and understands that he/she is the chosen channel for the success of the organization, no matter where they are in the hierarchy.

When you attain this mindset and your Mooladhara is invoked, you will enjoy selling more and see yourself in a state of flow. The flow that is perfect for the next Chakra - The Swadhisthana of Sales - your Creativity and Emotions.

THE SWADISTHANA / SACRAL CHAKRA OF CREATIVITY AND EMOTIONS

यद्यद्विभूतिमत्सत्त्वं श्रीमदूर्जितमेव वा।
तत्तदेवावगच्छ त्वं मम तेजोंऽशसंभवम्।।

Know that all opulent, beautiful, and glorious creations spring from but a spark of My splendor.

Chapter 10. Verse 41.

Swapna just won the Best Salesperson Award and she is over the moon. The hard work she put in has been rewarded.

As people congratulate her, they ask her to reveal how she could keep the momentum on in a difficult scenario. The majority of the people struggled to even get going while she surpassed expectations. It seems like she is truly in a state of flow at work.

She looks back at her journey and realizes how she created opportunities by being proactive and thinking out of the box. Her mindset shifted from being limited to knowing she can create unlimited opportunities to push her along. Unlike her colleagues, one thing that set her apart though was her ability to control her emotions and channelize her energy into things that mattered. She fueled her creativity by action and did not let her emotions get the best of her. The award is just a recognition of the fact that she is intelligent about her emotions and embraces her power to create. Be in a state of flow!

The state of flow is set forth by the right attitude; bringing with it great energy and vitality - almost life-giving.

Through the invocation of the root chakra of Sales, the Attitude, we can reach the place of creation and mastering our emotions.

Like the element of Water, the Chakra is attached to in Yoga, fluidity and adaptability will become second nature to you. In the last chapter, we did an exercise where you recollected an instance from your workplace in which you chose to put your head down and just go with the flow. If you are one of the people who experienced such a thing, you know the magic of your ability to be inactive in action begets.

When the mind is cluttered with thoughts beyond one's control - for example, the buying decision of a prospective customer, it blocks all energies to make things happen and to create opportunities.

On the *Kurukshetra*, Arjuna's success was not counted in terms of the number of soldiers killed. His success was measured with his commitment to his duties and doing whatever was necessary, without counting his achievements along the way.

He was a warrior meant to fulfill his duties on the battlefield. When he embraced this, he created strategies and manifested his most powerful *astras (weapons)*.

That power is what you need as a salesperson.

The power of creation.

Before I get to talking more about this, answer this question. Be aware, this question too like some previous ones are best answered when you think beyond what comes to you naturally as a salesperson. We are trying to kindle that inner self of yours that loves sales, but you may or may not know him/her yet!

REFLECTION TIME #4:

As a salesperson, what do you create?

____

____

____

____

____

____

____

Now that you have written the answer to the above question, go back and read the verse from the Bhagwad Gita at the beginning of this chapter. All that is beautiful and opulent is created by your splendor. I do not know exactly what you have written above. But most often than not, we know the power of selling and what we are creating. So, I assume what you have written is something that can be your vision statement. The answer to why you are selling.

Make this statement your driving force.

Let me give you a small example of how a simple statement can become your *mantra* for life and can open you up to infinite creative possibilities. Nelson Mandela, all through his imprisonment, lived by a particular line from the poem, Invictus by William Ernest Hemley. The lines were -

I am the master of my fate. I am the captain of my soul.

The Swadhisthana Chakra in Yoga and meditative practices are associated with adaptability and creativity. For us looking to be Sales Yogis, this Chakra is the doorway to infinite possibilities.

यच्चापि सर्वभूतानां बीजं तदहमर्जुन।
न तदस्ति विना यत्स्यान्मया भूतं चराचरम्।

I am the generating seed of all existences. There is no being - moving or nonmoving - that can exist without Me.

Chapter 10. Verse 39.

The essence of the above verse is that you have within you the power of creativity. For a salesperson, the possibilities are not limited to the database he/she has in the system. That is the mindset of a salesperson who yet doesn't know the power of being a *Karma Yogi.* You know it! Embrace that power.

If you look at any high achievers one thing that sets them apart is their ability to create. Create opportunities. Create needs. Create the aura around them that just attracts opulence. More often than not this wave of creativity is ridden on the surfboard of absolute surrender and dutifulness to the task at hand.

This gives us the power to create as we no longer are attached to the fruits and our emotions of happiness or distress.

The Swadhisthana of Sales is also the right place to get control of your emotions and regulate them. A lot has been spoken about emotions and emotional intelligence. The reason being, that is the one prison that is easiest to get into. The prison of your emotions, where you are controlled by it. The body gives out. The mind seems weak. It is especially one of the most important aspects of a salesperson. The emotional grit. This comes with a lot of practice and deep introspection. Understand that how you feel is directly correlated to how you choose to react to a situation. Modern-day positive psychologists say that close to 40-45% of what you feel is a direct result of what to choose for yourself in the situation. The Bhagwad Gita gives reference to twenty-four elements, inside and outside of us, that is called the field of activity.

महाभूतान्यहङ्कारो बुद्धिरव्यक्तमेव च।
इन्द्रियाणि दशैकं च पञ्च चेन्द्रियगोचराः।
इच्छा द्वेषः सुखं दुःखं सङ्घातश्चेतनाधृतिः।
एतत्क्षेत्रं समासेन सविकारमुदाहृतम्।।

The great elements, egoism, intellect, and also the Unmanifested Nature, the ten senses and one (mind), and the five objects of the senses. Desire, hatred, pleasure, pain, the aggregate (the body), intelligence, and fortitude. The field has thus been briefly described with its modifications.

Let us look at this verse in detail. This will be a very interesting take of the base emotions and how they interact with each other - taking you on a nonstop roller-coaster journey that begs for you to control it.

The above principles form the frame or the skeleton on which the world is built. All these are mental states and treated as properties of the body.

These are the inherent realities of the Self. The modifications have a beginning and an end. Only that which is unchanging can be the witness of these modifications. Let's look at some emotions that are mentioned as the important ones and form a part of the field of activity, as they can be known or observed. Just like the modern-day emotions wheel that many of us would have seen, from these twenty-four elements and their interaction in the world as we know it comes our emotions.

Look at Desire. Desire is a modification of the mind. It is an earnest longing for an object. It is a *Vritti (thought wave)* born of *Rajas* which urges a man who has once experienced a certain object of pleasure to get hold of it as conducive to his pleasure when he beholds the same object again. This is the property of the inner sense. It is the field because it is knowable. You enjoy a certain sensual object. The impression of this is produced in the subconscious mind. This impression is vivified or revived through memory or remembrance of sensual pleasure. Then desire arises to enjoy the object again. Repetition of sensual enjoyment intensifies memory and desire.

The memory of sensual enjoyments and the hearing of the alities of the sensual objects are the root causes of desires.

Desire excites the mind and the senses. Desire makes the mind restless. Desire makes the mind wander in the sensual grooves.

REFLECTION TIME #5:

Think of a time in your work, when you desired something so much you lost your mental and emotional balance. Think of what emotions you felt then and when you look back at them, what emotions do you feel now.

An object which is sweet and pleasant to you at one moment produces the very reverse of that sensation at another moment. Every one of you might have had this experience. Objects are pleasant only when there is a longing for them. But they are unpleasant when there is no longing for them. Therefore, desires are the cause of pleasure. If satisfaction arises through the enjoyment of the objects, pleasure will cease. Before economists coined the Law of Diminishing Marginal Utility, ancient philosophers of *Bharat* had figured this out - as Lord Krishna gave reference to in the Gita.

Now lets us take a look at one emotion that we as salespeople deal with often. Anger stemming from hatred or dislike to someone/ something. Hatred is a modification of the mind. It is a negative one. It is also a *Vritti* that impels a man who experienced pain from a certain object to dislike it when he beholds the same object again. Hatred also is a field because it is knowable. The modification that arises in the mind when your desire is not fulfilled is called hatred.

Similarly, pleasure is agreeable, peaceful - made of Sattva. This is also the field because it is knowable. Pain is disagreeable or unpleasant. It is also the field because it is knowable.

The emotionally intelligent look to identify their emotions, label them, and be unmoved by the emotions. In the last Reflection Time, you thought about a time at work where desire drove you to imbalance and feelings of negative emotions. Now when you look back at the incident, you can understand and unravel it much better. However, in the heat of when it was happening it must have been difficult to understand the absolute power that desire had on you.

It hence becomes very important to be able to understand what you feel and build a *Satvik* modification of the mind- *Dhriti (Firmness, Courage, Fortitude)* within.

The body, the senses, and the mind are sustained by this firmness when they are depressed and agitated - something that every salesperson can easily experience. Dhriti is firmness or the power by which a state of steadiness and balance is achieved. This is also the field because it is knowable.

If you can know it, you can control it.

BONUS#2
The Sales Yogi Swadhisthana Affirmation Statement:

I create great opportunities. I am a master of what and how I feel.

Summarizing some important elements that make up for mastering the Chakra of Creativity and Emotions for a Sales Yogi:

- The Sales Yogi enjoys the state of flow stemming from the attitude.
- Like water, the Sales Yogi is fluid and adaptable. Free in thoughts and emotions, the Sales Yogi is not bound or controlled by either.
- The Sales Yogi has the potential to create or shape his/her reality.
- The Sales Yogi strives to understand the emotions that operate in the field of activity and control his/her reaction to them.
- The Sales Yogi is firm and courageous in the face of distress or anger as he/she knows that is what will sustain.

With the power, the second chakra provides one can truly shine through. Many of the instances of burnout and disillusionment you may be facing in your work are more emotional and mental than physical. When you control your emotions and how you react to them, you keep the power with you - the power to create unlimited possibilities for yourself to shine and flourish. This power fires up the third chakra of Passion, Persistence, and Knowledge - *The Manipura.*

THE MANIPURA OF SALES - PASSION, PERSISTENCE, AND KNOWLEDGE

सत्त्वं रजस्तम इति गुणाः प्रकृतिसंभवाः।
निबध्नन्ति महाबाहो देहे देहिनमव्ययम्।।

Material Nature consists of three modes - goodness, passion, and ignorance. Born of nature these modes bind one and he becomes conditioned by them.

Chapter 14. Verse 5.

Hillary has been constantly working to get the best results for herself in the sales role.

However, she is not burnt out. She does not get excited about her work as much now. Her passion seems to have dwindled. Running mindlessly in the name of passion has caught up with her and she finds herself unable to persist and move ahead. Her product knowledge and her understanding of the market is also great. She is feeling the heat of losing her drive and that is troubling her.

She wonders what she did wrong in chasing her targets. A discussion with her boss helps her realize she feels this way because she did not channelize her energies properly.

A lot has been read and spoken about how passionate a salesperson needs to be. That fire in the belly! That "never say die" attitude. That blind race to keep the "fire burning." Until finally one burns out of fuel and is left clueless, like Hillary above.

I know that went south very quickly! There is a reason for that. It is the fact that we operate in three modes of Material Nature and that the mode in which we operate binds us to it. In this case, passion. What I will cover on passion and how a Sales Yogi sees it differently is different. The power of it is immense and it will need you to unlearn what you already know and see it in the new light of how the energy flows through the Seven Chakras of Sales.

The Third Chakra, Manipura, in Yoga translates to The City of Jewels. Jewels are forged by fire - the element that is associated with this chakra. In the world of sales, three jewels that let us shine are passion, persistence, and knowledge.

लोभः प्रवृत्तिरारम्भः कर्मणामशमः स्पृहा।
रजस्येतानि जायन्ते विवृद्धे भरतर्षभ।।

When there is an increase in the mode of passion the symptoms of great attachment, fruitive activities, intense endeavor, and uncontrollable desire and hankering develop.

Chapter 14. Verse 12.

We saw how desire is a negative modification of the elements and acts like quicksand - consuming us in it. One who is in the mode of passion as we traditionally know it is never satisfied with the accomplishments. While we all agree that one should always strive to get better, the fact remains that it is the attachment to these desires that spells doom.

A salesperson is always looking to better his/her position in the company, in the market, and the eyes of the customers. But if this desire is not controlled and monitored, it takes one on a spiraling journey - one that is more often than not a slide down than a climb up.

So how do we define passion as one of the jewels of the Manipura Chakra?

While passion is regarded as Rajas and is not the most desirable mode to be in, dutifulness is not. The root of our journey was exactly in cultivating this attitude. we also saw how when we were involved in work that was no longer something we approached as a task or a 'to-do' we attained the flow that opened up our power of creating opportunities.

Fame and success are the byproducts of the process you follow in Sales.

Let's take the example of how petrol is obtained from crude oil. The process of fractional distillation is a process of separating various fuels from the crude - helped by the element of fire. This process is a great example to understand where the fire needs to burn. It is not burning on the byproducts but the crude. What happens if the fire is placed below petrol (the outcome of the process)? It will burn away and in ample quantities will cause an explosion and destroy most things in its immediate radius.

The above verse from the Bhagwad Gita supports the same logic. That is why although passion helps you achieve things, it is not a mode that is permanent. But the trick to make it last longer is to focus your energies on the processes you have set for yourself to help and enable you in selling faster and more. The love for your duty as a salesperson. The ability to keep the focus on lighting the fire where it matters the most and enjoy the benefits of it.

REFLECTION TIME#6:

When you were previously told to be passionate, where did you immediately turn your attention to? Think of it in terms of why you started doing things and if you did or did not achieve what you set out to do. If you did achieve what you set out to do, were you content after you achieved that milestone, or did the hankering for more kick in?

As we strive to keep the fire burning through the wood of our passion, the other jewel that gains importance is persistence. The air to the fire. The second jewel in the three jewels of the Manipura of Sales.

A quick search on how Persistence is defined will show you that it is the fact of continuing in an opinion or course of action despite difficulty or opposition. Tie this back to whatever you have read in this book till now and you realize that all those aspects are helping you to be more persistent.

The key here is to answer this question:

REFLECTION TIME#7:

Where in the sales process and procedures you follow can you be persistent?

____

____

____

____

____

____

____

Without seeing your responses to the above question, I can say with utmost confidence that everything you think you can be persistent about is something that you can do or think. Things that you control. What does that say about persistence in sales?

It says very clearly that when you are passionate about what needs to be done to achieve your goals you add life to that fire by being persistent about the various steps in the process. It is a direct correlation and the beauty of it is that what you can be consistent about is always what you control. Can you be persistent about the client's decision? You cannot. But you can be persistent about the follow-up. The reason why in every sales training program this aspect is repeated.

The power of discipline and consistency is often underrated. In the cycle of happiness and distress as and when you win and lose deals, you may forget to give the due credit to the discipline that took you there in the first place. Highly successful salespeople have systems and processes working for them. Through their persistence and consistency, they break the cycle of emotional distress and stand steady and unperturbed by the cyclical nature of sales - much like the cyclical nature of the seasons.

मात्रास्पर्शास्तु कौन्तेय शीतोष्णसुखदुःखदाः।
आगमापायिनोऽनित्यास्तांस्तितिक्षस्व भारत।।

The nonpermanent appearance of happiness and distress, and their disappearance in due course, are like the appearance and disappearance of winter and summer seasons. They arise from sense perception, O scion of Bharata, and one must learn to tolerate them without being disturbed.

Chapter 2. Verse 14.

The keywords in the above verse are 'learn to tolerate.' None of us are immune to the highs and the lows of sales, but learning to be steady matters. The last chapter covered the aspect of emotions and we saw in its summary how the Sales Yogi works continuously to master the emotions and understand them better.

Persistence or patience is referred to as one of the seven opulence in the Bhagwad Gita and one who possesses it will always taste glory. When we looked at the steps in your sales process where you are consistent, that gave you a blueprint of areas that you passionately need to ensure gets done. Knowing which steps and processes will help you succeed is an important lesson you teach yourself. While what each of you sells may be different what does not change is the fact that you know what you are selling and then set up processes for selling that you follow with passion.

Knowledge is the third jewel in the Manipura of Sales. Without the knowledge of what, why, and how you are selling, it is a blind race to nowhere. Most companies and teams spend a lot of time empowering you with knowledge about the company and the products and/or services. For the Sales Yogi, the jewel of knowledge is more intrinsic, as you would have already figured out from the tone of this book.

Many of you have already invested time and effort in gaining knowledge about the skills required to be effective in sales. I have touched upon previously in this chapter about the importance of disciplining yourself to follow the tips, tricks, and processes.

For this jewel of Knowledge, we will look at the various qualities listed down in the Bhagwad Gita and their importance in sales.

बुद्धिर्ज्ञानमसंमोहः क्षमा सत्यं दमः शमः।

सुखं दुःखं भवोऽभावो भयं चाभयमेव च।।

अहिंसा समता तुष्टिस्तपो दानं यशोऽयशः।

भवन्ति भावा भूतानां मत्त एव पृथग्विधाः।।

Intelligence, knowledge, freedom from doubt and delusion, forgiveness, truthfulness, control of the senses, control of the mind, happiness and

distress, birth, death, fear, fearlessness, nonviolence, equanimity, satisfaction, austerity, charity, fame and infamy - all these various qualities of living beings are created by Me alone.

Chapter 10. Verses 4 and 5.

As you read the above verse, you can paint the picture of what qualities matter. It is this knowledge that is important as these aspects govern all that we are taught and conditioned to.

The academic knowledge we gain is limited. Limited to the product. Limited to the process. Limited to the company. However, we did cover how to use this limited knowledge and turn it into the fuel that lights the fire in your belly. Further here I attempt to pass on the knowledge of the various qualities and their impact on us.

Intelligence

This quality refers to the power to analyze things from the right perspective. our education sets us up for imbibing this quality. This pertains only to matter though and is not complete. But it is important nonetheless. All the training you have gone through to understand more about the features, USPs, value, and vision are aimed at making you intelligent enough to handle the objections you face in the sales cycle. Without this knowledge, you are powerless.

Knowledge

Knowledge in the form of matter is ordinary according to the Bhagwad Gita. True knowledge is knowing the difference between spirit and matter. That is where this quality becomes more intrinsic to you. While this knowledge is metaphysical, we look at this aspect as knowing oneself better. The spirit which dwells in this vessel of your body is meant to sell. Put in the time and effort to know yourself better. Work on the weaknesses and solidify the strengths. That will put you on the path of continuous learning - one of the key learning objectives in companies, especially for salespeople.

Freedom from Doubt and Delusion (Asammoha)

This is a quality that is characterized by action. Not hesitating to fulfill what is your duty. When you shine through your action, you remove any donut or delusion in your mind. It grants you freedom as an individual and as a salesperson from any impeding thoughts or emotions you may have in your mind.

Tolerance and Forgiveness - Kshama

The grind of sales is an easy place to lose your balance and calm. Knowing your triggers and working towards arresting them is a significant step forward in your Sales Yogi journey. This is a quality that you should consciously practice. Be tolerant and excuse the setbacks, minor offenses of others, and anything else that your work in sales will throw at you.

Truthfulness (Satyam)

I had a joke that was forwarded to me once. It had the scene of an interview where the interviewer is hiring for a sales position. Written on it were the words, "Everything in your resume is a lie. Welcome to sales!" Naturally, I was not very happy about the joke but this is something salespeople do unintentionally. The fallacy of saying what the prospects want to hear is the cause of this impression of sales and salespeople. Truthfulness means the presentation of facts, as they are, for the benefit of others. Say the truth to your customers and your managers, and not what is palatable. Removal of the notion that truth should only be spoken when it is palatable is necessary. We will be covering the aspect of speech in one of the other Chakras.

Control of the Mind and Senses (Sama)

We live in a distracted world. More so now with virtual becoming a reality. There are many things on hand for the salesperson in his/her day. The last thing you need is to have your senses become a distraction too. While you cannot switch off these sense organs, you can still control and regulate what and how much you intake. The biggest culprit in all these is the mind. The bonus chapters on meditation and Yoga will arm you with the necessary insights to master this quality of a self-realized salesperson

Happiness (Sukham)

This is one word that triggers many reactions. While Happiness is subjective there are certain effective guidelines for you to ensure you derive pleasure from what you do in sales. The most important one is to train yourself with the knowledge of what is favorable for you and what is unfavorable for you as emotions and thoughts. When the highly anticipated deal goes to a competitor, you can feel the pinch for a bit. But you will then have to decide if you want to keep sulking or move ahead and get back to being a *Karma Yogi.*

Fear and Fearlessness (Bhayam and Abhayam)

One of the greatest fears we deal with as salespeople are the fear of rejection or being ghosted by the prospect. Yet again the energy of fear stems from illusion. In the Bhagwad Gita, it is clearly stated that fear is illusory energy. Once you realize this, armed with the other aspects like client centricity and communication, which we will look at in the upcoming chapters, you will be able to be more fearless. Always remember, if you do not ask you do not get.

Equanimity (Samata)

The dictionary definition of equanimity is the quality to remain calm in difficult situations. Isn't this one of the most important things for anyone, let alone a salesperson, to learn? The Bhagwad Gita goes ahead and tells you that this equanimity is something that will keep you on the path to your goals. The reason being, you take the power into your hands by practicing this quality of being calm. You choose to deal with any difficult situation with grace and fortitude.

Austerity (Tapas)

The penance you undertake as a salesperson is to keep doing your duty even when you don't want to sometimes. We covered the aspect of persistence earlier in this chapter. But Tapas is necessary to discipline yourself to be able to go through the ups and downs of sales with ease. It doesn't matter how you feel about things that affect you, but you need to do this penance. This will empower you to remove roadblocks in your work.

Fame (Yashas)

The biggest result of a job well done. Pat on the backs. Incentives, Glory! Fame is like a drug and you can get consumed by it. Hankering for more like we saw earlier is always going to land you in distress and delusion. The real fame for a salesperson is not when he/she consistently hits his target. The real fame is when the customer accepts him/her as their most preferred partner. Something that is only achieved by keeping the client in your hearts.

That is the next Chakra but we will keep it for then. Let's summarize what we covered here.

BONUS#3
The Sales Yogi Manipura Affirmation Statement:

I am powerful and steadfast. My light shines through my knowledge of myself and beyond.

- The Sales Yogi knows his three jewels are his passion, persistence, and knowledge.
- The Sales Yogi realizes channelizing passion is important as it has the quality to burn like fire.
- The Sales Yogi understands that everything that makes him/her persistent is always something he/she can control.
- The Sales Yogi knows that knowledge of academia is just half knowledge. True power comes from self-realization.
- The Sales Yogi concentrates on certain qualities that are important and strives to increase his/her knowledge on these aspects to empower themselves.

There are a few more qualities that are mentioned in the Bhagwad Gita but may not be relevant to what the book tries to uncover. As we saw earlier, the true fame for a salesperson is born out of love for the customer. Every sale has two parties coming together and the customer is someone who you cannot strike down. Like Anahata, the next Chakra of Client Centric Mindset which translates to the "unstruck."

THE ANAHATA OF SALES - CLIENT CENTRICITY

गतिर्भर्ता प्रभुः साक्षी निवासः शरणं सुहृत्।
प्रभवः प्रलयः स्थानं निधानं बीजमव्ययम्।।

I am the goal, the supporter, the Lord, the witness,
the abode, the shelter, the friend, the origin, the
dissolution, the foundation, the treasure-house,
and the seed which is imperishable.

Chapter 9. Verse 18.

Prakash is loved by all his clients. His teammates often wonder what his magic trick is.

He recalls a very specific event in his career where a potential customer was just not happy with the way he dealt with the client's queries. As he enquired for features within the product that the ready offering did not have, Prakash had said no to the possibility of exploring a solution right away.

This irked the customer and he instructed Prakash to get the CEO the next time he went to discuss with the client. Then Prakash had to step back and see the other take over the conversations. The greatest learning he had that day was that he did not ask the right question to understand why the client would have such a need.

Prakash says he lost a partnership with his client that day and so he now keeps the client at the center of every conversation.

How apt is the above verse the moment you think of the power within your *Anahata* - Client Centricity!

Whatever you do, the goal is to get a customer, isn't it?

That is where our roads lead to. Customers support our businesses. They are the witness to our products and services. They become our friends. All our efforts originate and end with them. They are the true treasure house for us, not only in terms of money but also in terms of the immense experience and stories we can gather while working with them. What is sold may perish but the buyer always stays.

Such is the importance of your client. Your customer.

The first step to understanding this is to know while the customer need not always be right, you will always need to be right for the customer.

Read that again.

Knowing what is right is not enough. You will need to do right for your customer. Client-Centric Mindset is not only important after a sale is made. It starts from the first call made to a cold prospect and remains "unstruck" all through the lifetime of the customer's association with you and your company.

Like air which this chakra is symbolized within Yoga, your Anahata of Client Centricity signifies the love you will have to serve your customers. Energetically, Anahata helps you tap into unconditional love. For all salespeople, there is no purer love than serving the customer. Maybe I am sounding too poetic, but that is the truth.

तेषां ज्ञानी नित्ययुक्त एकभक्तिर्विशिष्यते।
प्रियो हि ज्ञानिनोऽत्यर्थमहं स च मम प्रियः।।

Of them, the man of Knowledge, endowed with constant steadfastness and one-pointed devotion, excels. For I am very much dear to the man of Knowledge, and he too is dear to Me.

Chapter 7. Verse 17.

Three key elements in the above verse are knowledge, steadfastness (persistence), and one-pointed devotion (passion)! Pleasantly surprised? The aspects we covered in the last chapter open your heart up to the devotion you will need to succeed in your client interactions. In my sales journey, I have seen too many sales talent go to waste because of the inability to put the customer first. In the hustle and bustle of sales, the one thing that separates the great from the good is how well you can build and maintain mutually beneficial relations. When we look at the Bhagwad Gita many things the book speaks about revolve around the theme of devotional service. All that we touched upon in the previous chapters too have this germinating idea. The reason being, that is the seat to higher intelligence - what we saw in the last chapter is true knowledge.

REFLECTION TIME #8:

Recall an instance from your work where your customer was not happy with you. This could be for whatsoever reason. Write it down below. Do not judge yourself. The idea is to understand what you feel went wrong. When you write it down, it becomes clearer and more present and thus easier to unlearn and overcome.

____

____

____

____

____

____

____

Lord Krishna answers Arjuna's request to see him in his true form by revealing that everything this universe is made up of is fragments of him. Starting from the smallest of atoms to the _Vishwaroopam_ (universal form) that contains within itself everything we know and beyond. If you ask the successful salespeople all around what was a key factor in their growth, most of them will talk about how they gave importance to every customer that ever came their way - from the smallest to the biggest. Such unwavering devotion to your customer is what you need. The central theme of many chapters within the Bhagwad Gita.

Bhakti Yoga. Devotional Service.

The term Bhakti is often used in matters of faith. For us to understand it in the context of what sales are, it is important to look at it from a different angle. The angle of customer-centricity. At the very beginning of the book we answered the question - Why do you sell? Most of what you must have written in terms of the larger impact would have some solution or impact you deliver to your customer.

The sixteenth chapter in the Bhagwad Gita lays down a comparison between what is divine and demoniac. One particular verse stood out to me and I am sharing it here.

आढ्योऽभिजनवानस्मि कोऽन्योऽस्ति सदृशो मया।
यक्ष्ये दास्यामि मोदिष्य इत्यज्ञानविमोहिताः।।

The demoniac person thinks: "So much wealth do I have today, and I will gain more according to my schemes. So much is mine now, and it will increase in the future, more and more. He is my enemy and I have killed him, and my other enemies will also be killed. I am the lord of everything. I am the enjoyer. I am perfect,

**powerful, and happy. I am the richest, surrounded by aristocratic relatives. There is none so powerful and happy as I am. I shall perform sacrifices. I shall give some charity, and thus I shall rejoice."
In this way, such persons are deluded by ignorance.**

Chapter 16. Verse 16.

As you read the above verse if you were to interact with someone who epitomizes all that the verse says, what will be your reaction to him/her? Think about it for a while.

The seat of goodness that I have been speaking about has its intention of making you a person the client would love to interact with. Important qualities of empathy and devotion are of utmost importance. Robert K. Greenleaf coined the philosophy of Servant Leadership in 1994. He did not define it as leadership and service is always in flux. However, the concept also says that what is needed is a spiritual understanding of identity, mission, vision, and environment.

When you look at it every salesperson is a servant leader. Sales is a high-touch profession where every day there is human interaction and in the center of it all is our customer. You are leading them on a journey with you where your devotion to serving will determine the distance you go with them. Needless to say, this will require you to imbibe some characteristics which will invoke the Anahata within you. I am highlighting them below.

Listen more. Speak less.

The first and the most important thing to do to be client-centric. Do you remember the story I shared from my interaction with a client earlier in the chapter? The thing that was missing there was the intention to listen. Though we did work with the customer and he became one of our patrons eventually, I would say I was lucky. If you do not listen, you cannot sell.

Be Empathetic

The mode of goodness! The Bhagwad Gita speaks out the three modes of material nature and says how striving to be in the mode of goodness is the only way to transcend and move up in life. Empathy is the ability to sense and understand the feelings of others. We touched upon understanding and controlling our emotions in the second chapter of this book. But for a true Sales Yogi who embodies client centricity, empathy is the greatest strength.

Own Up!

The Bhagwad Gita says it is better to be devoted to one's occupation and do it imperfectly than to accept another's occupation and do it perfectly.

What does this mean? In the grind of sales, we all tend to lose ownership of what our roles entail. With some setbacks come excuses that give you the false belief that the fault is with others or the stars (luck). While in some cases it may also be true, but a man of action takes the ownership and makes attempts to turn it around. When you serve your customer in *Bhakti Yog*, you take full responsibility for their experience.

Be a Change Agent

As a salesperson, you may be holding the power to change the narrative for the stories of your clients. In sales by asking the right questions and listening to what the client says helps us bring change and impact the lives of others. Know that when a prospect is interested in something you pitch, your objective immediately should be to understand how you can create an impact for them than thinking about how you can increase your sales numbers. It is a difficult thing to do in the high-pressure role of being a salesperson but like I said earlier in the chapter, the best of salespeople are the ones that have kept the client in their hearts.

Effectively Conceptualize

Solutions are what you talk about when you sell to your customer. What is the pain point you solve? How does your product/service make life better for your customer? Your ability to conceptualize these things will help you be a better salesperson. When you can share the vision of your company and believe in the product or service, articulate how you can help your customer, and communicate effectively to lead them through the journey, your interactions will become more positive and impactful.

REFLECTION TIME #9:

Write down how you are going to imbibe the five qualities highlighted above to be more client-centric. Make them actionable points. Do not create statements that are vague like - "I will listen more." Think of HOW you will do that and note those points down for the five qualities.

____

____

____

____

____

____

____

____

BONUS #4:
The Sales Yogi Anahata Affirmation Statement:

I am the seat of goodness for my customers. Through me, they grow and change.

- The Sales Yogi is devoted to his customer.
- The Sales Yogi builds and nurtures relationships.
- The Sales Yogi understands the concept of Bhakti Yoga and strives to practice it every day.
- The Sales Yogi knows he/she holds the power within to impact and do good.
- The Sales Yogi Imbibes the five key qualities that will lead him to be a preferred partner to his/her clients.

Having reached this Chakra of sales, we open ourselves to the external world more. Progressively learning about the true essence of the four chakras we already covered, we now get to the one that stamps our authority and creates what we now call our "personal brand." The Vishuddha of Sales - the chakra of Communication and Expression.

THE VISHUDDHA OF SALES - COMMUNICATION AND EXPRESSION

मृत्युः सर्वहरश्चाहमुद्भवश्च भविष्यताम्।
कीर्तिः श्रीर्वाक्च नारीणां स्मृतिर्मेधा धृतिः क्षमा।।

I am all-devouring death, and I am the generating principle of all that is yet to be. Among the feminine alities (I am) fame, prosperity, speech, memory, intelligence, firmness, and forgiveness.

Chapter 10. Verse 34.

Shravya has been having trouble getting the prospects and clients to listen to her.

She is excellent in her diction and speech but yet fails to connect with the client in a way that will increase her influence on them. Shravya is at her wit's end when she asks her dearest friend Samvritha what she thinks is the missing link.

Samvritha immediately responds and tells her that she never pauses to listen. In sales, listening is a very important aspect and if Shravya is not going to allow the other person to speak more than she does, the conversations in all likelihood will not progress to closure for her. Samvritha further adds that when she started pausing and listening, she was able to ask more powerful questions and understand what the customer needs better. She says is it time Shravya starts this purification process in her communication. The process of Vishuddha.

The power of this chakra is infinite much like the element it is associated with, in Yoga - Space (Ether).

With the energetic function of speaking and authentic self-expression, it is no surprise that this chakra for sales is all about Communication and Expression.

The first line of the verse with which the chapter started perfectly sums up the importance of communication in sales. Struggle with your communication and ability to express yourself and in all probabilities, the opportunity dies. But master the art of self-expression and communication and you will see every seed you have planted germinate and take shape.

In our day and age communication is also often attached to your command over a language. While that is important, the key thing to know is the art of expressing what you want to say. From your pitches to the trickiest negotiations. Effective communication is a must-have skill for salespeople. When you can send the intended message in an intended way to the right person you effectively communicate. Fine speech is described as one of the opulence in the Bhagwad Gita. If a person possesses this, he becomes glorious! Now, who wouldn't want to be a glorious salesperson? Speech (communication) has also been given the place of an austerity (Tapas or Rigor) in the Bhagwad Gita. It says:

अनुद्वेगकरं वाक्यं सत्यं प्रियहितं च यत्।

स्वाध्यायाभ्यसनं चैव वाङ्मयं तप उच्यते।।

Austerity of speech consists of speaking words that are truthful, pleasing, beneficial, and not agitating to others, and also in regularly reciting Vedic literature.

Chapter 17. Verse 15.

Let's break down the above verse and you will see a few key things stand out when it comes to fine-tuning your speech.

Be authentic.

Truthfulness in your words will go a long way to establish the credibility you seek in the eyes of your customers. Nothing that is layered with a coating of lies lasts. If the wrong commitment has been given to the customer, sooner or later you will face the consequences of not being truthful in your communication. The repercussions may be internal or external to your organization. But there will always be an outcome. When that happens your authenticity in communication will determine your credibility.

Be pleasing.

This doesn't mean sugar coating! The essence of being pleasing is to enable the other person to want to listen to you speak and express. If you can be soft-spoken and courteous then it becomes that much easier to get the attention of the other person. Even the harshest of truths can be said pleasingly and not necessarily in a curt manner. It is an aspect that you will master through a lot of practice. The mark of an effective communicator is also that the person to whom the message is sent receives the message with the exact intention it was sent out. Remember, it is a two-way street!

Be beneficial.

When you are truthful and courteous in your communication, you elevate yourself to a position of a benefactor. The wealth of giving the right and important information through your communication cannot be measured. Speak to impact positively. In sales, this becomes one of the most important things to understand and imbibe. When you communicate to benefit others, you radiate authenticity.

Be non-agitating.

Similar to being courteous, it is important to be non-agitating in your speech. Words have the power to be the all-devouring death. More often than not people forget actions but seldom do they forget words. Words touch hearts and invoke emotions. In the field of sales, there is no room for making anyone feel offended or agitated. The term aggressive salesperson needs to be seen in how you are being a Karma Yogi and not in words that you use to communicate and connect with your stakeholders.

Be knowledgeable

The analogy of Vedic literature in the above verse is related to academic knowledge. it will not matter if you are truthful, courteous, beneficial, and non-agitating if what you say doesn't make any sense to the person listening. That is one of the top reasons why salespeople are given pitches and product features list and many other documents. Imagine sitting in front of the client with the best of intentions but no knowledge of your offering.

In the modern-day concepts too, you will find similar guidelines laid down to achieve effective communication. Let's see one definition of Effective Communication -

Effective Communication is a communication between two or more persons wherein the intended message is successfully delivered, received, and understood.

In my research on this topic, I came across a great article on one of the sites* and it laid down a few of the barriers to effective communication. The barriers to effective communication can be divided broadly into four categories:

Semantic Barriers: What you say and show need not be the same as the other person understands that word or symbol as. This difference may cause semantic barriers.

Psychological or Emotional Barriers: The opinions, attitudes, emotions, status consciousness, etc. all add to this barrier in communication.

Organizational Barriers: As the name suggests, this is intrinsic to the organization and hinders the flow of information in it.

Personal Barriers: Personal barriers are factors that are personal to the sender or receiver of communication.

While organizational barriers are outside the scope of this book, let's further analyze the other three barriers.

Semantic barriers arise out of differences in how a word or image can be interpreted. This can be because of many factors like failing to express properly, a bad translation, usage of too many technical jargons, using symbols and words that may have different meanings, unclarified assumptions, and knowing the difference between denotations and connotations. Your ability to see these barriers and overcome them will help make the communication more effective.

Personal and Emotional / Psychological barriers are something I am aiming for you to overcome in this chapter. Barriers like low attention, judgmental mindset, a poor memory arising out of distractions, lack of trust, and your emotions are all detrimental.

When you communicate with someone the focus is to give him/her your full attention and time.

This brings us to yet another art that we have all heard many times as something we need to master. The Art of Listening.

मय्यासक्तमनाः पार्थ योगं युञ्जन्मदाश्रयः।
असंशयं समग्रं मां यथा ज्ञास्यसि तच्छृणु।।

The Blessed Lord said - O Partha, how by practicing yoga in full consciousness of Me, with mind attached to Me, you can know Me in full, free from doubt.

Chapter 7. Verse 1.

When you are fully engrossed in the conversation and you attach yourself to the other person in the conversation, you will start listening more and talking less. Arjuna asks not many questions in the Bhagwad Gita. But he listens intently. His intent listening is the reason that Lord Krishna opens up and starts speaking more about transcendental knowledge. The knowledge that has lasted for ages and has inspired this attempt to combine it with modern-day sales too.

The power that listening gives you is the power of realized knowledge.

इदं तु ते गुह्यतमं प्रवक्ष्याम्यनसूयवे।
ज्ञानं विज्ञानसहितं यज्ज्ञात्वा मोक्ष्यसेऽशुभात्।।

The Blessed Lord said I shall now declare to thee who does not cavil, the greatest secret, the knowledge combined with experience (Self-realisation). Having known this thou shalt be free evil.

Chapter 9. Verse 1.

Cavil is an interesting word. Cavil means to make petty and unnecessary objections. Look back at what many salespeople are guilty of. They are guilty of talking more and listening less. They cavil to gain the upper hand only to realize that it was not needed at all. Imagine the opposite of this. What if you had a conversation that was just flowing and effortless? As you strike through the words and see the prospect opening up more and more information for you to gather. You progress from an introduction to an actual need in the first call itself. Now, wouldn't that be just perfect?

The Bhagwad Gita starts with an introduction to the aspects covered in the book and slowly progresses to concepts of Karma Yogi and devotional service before reaching the ninth chapter, which like the above verse says is the greatest secret. What I am trying to highlight here is that Lord Krishna says this openly to Arjuna that because he is listening intently, he will get more knowledge.

With the importance of listening reinforced let us also see how we can practice this in our communication. These are a few things I have learned from my experience in sales. There are many more elements in the art of listening but through proactive I have narrowed down on these six.

Listen to Feel

What I mean by this is to practice listening to emotions rather than words. The tone of the voice, the eye contact, the body language, etc. are all pointers to the underlying emotions of what is being said. This is also important to make that connection with the other person. If the emotion with which the communication is sent and the emotion with which the communication is received isn't similar, it immediately creates a disconnect.

Slow down

To do the above, the next step is to slow down the conversation. Do not be in a rush to speak everything at the word go. Create conversations and go ahead at a slow and composed pace and not at the speed of light! Salespeople are full of ideas and emotions and that can mean communication that is so fast, the other person doesn't get anything that is being said. Even your elevator pitch can be delivered at a composed pace. Just need to get your words right!

Interrupt and be Ignored

One golden rule to better listening. DO NOT INTERRUPT. Be patient and let the other person finish what is being said. Our minds are processing responses even before we hear what the other person is saying. You may be losing out on important things that the prospect or customer may be saying just because you interjected. Continue this and no one will like to speak to you and soon all your calls will be ignored. Another useful hack is to pause after the other person has finished speaking. When you do that more often than not, they will have something to add to what has already been saying.

Summarizing

A salesperson needs to summarize the conversation before ending it. If there are no takeaways it is going to be just an exchange of information. If the intention of the conversation was that. But if you are looking to sell and be useful for your customer, you will need to clarify any doubts you may have and then paraphrase the conversation. This will help the other person also know you are carrying ahead the information in the exact manner as intended. You don't look foolish by repeating and summarizing what has already been spoken.

Show your stories

Don't tell. Show. How many times have we come across this statement? In the Bhagwad Gita, Lord Krishna could have just spoken about the glory of his Vishwaroopam (Universal Form). He chose to show it to Arjuna. The power of stories is compounded if you can paint images in the minds of the prospect/customer as you speak. The key to doing this to never forget your anecdotes. They make you stand out and can be very useful in breaking the ice. Ask more questions about the person and do not just approach as a lead. Make proper notes. These will serve as friendly references the next time you speak to them and you will be able to build a great rapport with them. After all, people love doing business with people.

Ask Questions

The magic of being in sales is that we truly possess the ability to solve problems with the products and services we sell. We have seen this in the previous chapters too. But you are not going to know what the problem is if you just assume it to be exactly in line with the "why" of your product. Asking the right questions is extremely critical for this and you all know the importance of it. the tweak I would recommend if you're not already doing it is to have the questions for your prospect/customer at the beginning of the conversation. Remember to never assume anything when you ask questions. Even if you think you know the answer, listen to it intently and be open to what is being said.

REFLECTION TIME #10:

After every call, think back and analyze how you listened to the other person. When you intentionally critique your conversations, you empower yourself to become better. There is no better tool for learning than self-realization. Keep doing this over the next ten calls you may have. Try to progressively improve in each of your conversations with the reflections you have made. Write down the key changes you made that enabled you to be a better listener after the tenth call.

____

____

____

____

____

____

____

BONUS #5:
The Sales Yogi Vishuddha Affirmation Statement:

I speak to be authentic. I listen to inspire change.

- The Sales Yogi is truthful and authentic in speech.
- The Sales Yogi strives to be courteous and puts the interest of the other person ahead in a conversation.
- The Sales Yogi looks to constantly improve the art of effective communication through practice and observation.
- The Sales Yogi understands that fine speech is as much a gift as it is a penance.
- The Sales Yogi listened intently and without cavil.
- The Sales Yogi identifies the personal and emotional barriers and puts them aside to make communication mutually beneficial.

When you purify yourself with the practices we covered in this chapter, you transcend to being someone who radiates goodness. The ripples of being a great communicator are that it opens you up to higher possibilities and like the space element associated with this chakra those could be infinite. It is one of those things that will elevate you and keep elevating you as there is no end to how much you can gain and learn through the art of communication and listening. This perfectly sets you up for gaining higher knowledge. The knowledge of self-realization. Your intuition.

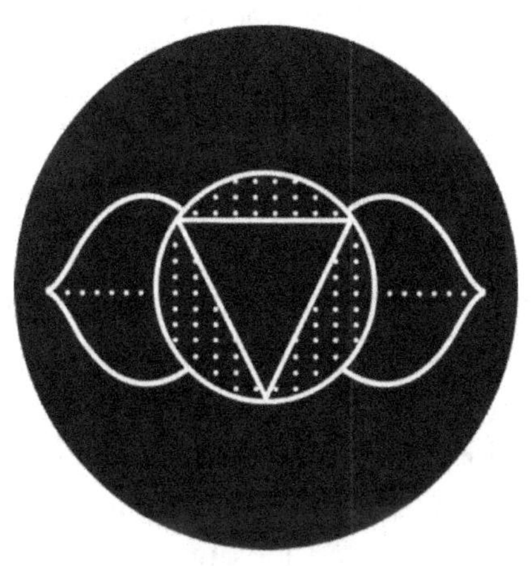

THE AJNA OF SALES - INTUITION AND OPENNESS

श्रुतिविप्रतिपन्ना ते यदा स्थास्यति निश्चला।
समाधावचला बुद्धिस्तदा योगमवाप्स्यसि।।

When your mind is no longer disturbed by the flowery language of the Vedas, and when it remains fixed in the trance of self-realization, then you have attained divine consciousness.

Chapter 2. Verse 53

Raghu is regretting not listening to his inner voice earlier. A quarter earlier he had been given the opportunity of investing time into a new market that the company wanted him to lead.

His gut had told him that this was a great opportunity but he did not want to leave his comfort zone and grow. The mind was closed then and he realizes that now. Luckily for Raghu, when the realization struck him that he should take up the new opportunity, it was not too late. It has been a month since he started looking at the new market with a more open view and that has shown him results.

Yes, he does feel it would have been great to have taken the opportunity earlier, but his path to understanding that required him to trust his gut. Now that he has done it, he says he is in a trance.

The trance of self-realization!

Such an amazing thing to even think about. Intuition is something that we all are familiar with. But what most do not know is that it is a powerful tool in your self-development journey. As it is one powerful tool for you to grow as a person, its importance in the field of sales and your daily interactions is also high.

The Ajna Chakra of Sales is your Intuition and Openness.

The word Ajna means the command center. That is what your intuition does. It is your inner guidance system. It guides you, nudges you, and prevents you from making the wrong decisions. Every one of us is born with this "sixth sense." In the Yoga philosophy, the Ajna chakra is not associated with any element as it is considered to be beyond the physical elements. It is the chakra to self-realization and knowing oneself better - emotionally, mentally, and spiritually.

इन्द्रियाणि पराण्याहुरिन्द्रियेभ्यः परं मनः।
मनसस्तु परा बुद्धिर्यो बुद्धेः परतस्तु सः।।

The working senses are superior to the dull matter; the mind is higher than the senses; intelligence higher than the mind; and the soul is even higher than the intelligence.

Chapter 3. Verse 42.

It is the progression from your physical senses to the subconscious mind that will power the intuition within you. For a salesperson, the gut feeling or the hunch turns out to be true more often than not. Let's do a small exercise:

REFLECTION TIME #11:

Choose a nice quiet spot to do this reflection. Close your eyes. Breathe in and out and bring the focus to your breath. When you feel calm, think about one instance where you followed your gut feeling and it helped you. As you do that try to look for the reasons why you followed your gut in that instance. Be with the thoughts for some time. Now open your eyes and write them down here.

____

____

____

____

____

____

____

Did you realize how your intuition guided you in the above experience in selling?

As we move further in the chapter, I will uncover some proven ways to strengthen this inner voice and get it to start working for you. This is not a concept that is just metaphysical but many successful people have embraced and developed their intuition to guide them in tough situations. If you would like people to listen to you and follow you then the first thing you need to do is start listening to yourself.

The word intuition is derived from the Latin word Intueri that means "look into." The quick insight you have before rational analysis and deductive thinking kicks in. The key is to be able to listen to this voice as and when it comes up. I am listing below some ways of harnessing and strengthening your intuition below. Have learned these through my Happiness Coaching practice and the many hours of research on these subjects. Practice these every day to flex that grey matter!

Disclaimer: Do not do these when you are in conversation with a potential client or a customer.

Living in the Now

That is correct. As the many life principles that make us happier and content, living in the present moment is ranked right up there. The modern-day principle of Mindfulness talks about this as a subject in itself. When you are in the moment without much attachment to the past or the future, you truly can experience peace and with that increase the power to listen to your voice. Picture a meeting where both you and the other person keep talking without much attention. In the noise that is created, both your voices die down. Similarly, for you to be able to listen to your inner voice, you need to shut out the voice of the past and the future in your mind. At work, practicing the concept of Karma Yogi will help you with this.

Mother Nature is the best

We truly belong in Nature and its abundant supply of life and positivity. Time you spend with nature will help you unplug almost on a daily basis. I start my day with fifteen minutes of silence in my balcony. Where the only thing I savor are the smells and sounds of the dawn. Like I mentioned in the very first chapter in this book, rise up early to spend an undisturbed time with yourself and Mother Nature first thing in the morning. This will set you up spiritually and mentally for your duty of sales in the day.

Feeling Low?

It is also important to know when you are feeling low and when you are feeling high. Your energy levels may not be the same always. Your inner voice loses its power when you crowd your mind with negativity or surround yourself with negative people. In the world of sales, bad news is generally a daily challenge to deal with. When you feel low, take a break. Listen to your feelings. Understand them and then choose to react in a positive way. Intuition flourishes where positivity resides.

Journaling

This is one thing most mindfulness practitioners or counsellors will tell their clients to do. Writing down the thoughts as and when they occur without judging them. Your journal will be the document of your inner self. Reading and writing leave a better imprint on your mind than just flowing through your thoughts. It also gives you an opportunity to revisit the thoughts and emotions at a later stage and thereby feeding your intuition to warn you or guide you the next time you come across a similar situation - and in sales we face the same situations many times.

Meditation

Physical exercise for the mind! That is what meditation is. There are many forms of meditation and you should try a few to understand what works for you best. While I am a daily practitioner of meditation, I am certainly not an expert in giving you tips on how to meditate. What I can say for certain is that when you meditate you for sure pay attention to feelings and thoughts that you may normally pay no heed to. Meditation helps you in clearing the fog of thoughts and reaching into your intuitive self. It is similar to switching on the defogger to clear the fog gathered on your car's windscreen. As the cloud clears, you are able to see clearer and farther.

My intention here is to get you to understand the value of Intuition in your self-realization journey. While some are gifted with the "hunch" modern psychology has proven that it is something that can be developed through practice. In the Bhagwad Gita, there is one whole chapter on Dhyan Yoga. The way of a Yogi.

बन्धुरात्माऽऽत्मनस्तस्य येनात्मैवात्मना जितः।
अनात्मनस्तु शत्रुत्वे वर्तेतात्मैव शत्रुवत्।।

For him who has conquered the mind, the mind is the best of friends; but for one who has failed to do so, his mind will remain the greatest enemy.

Chapter 6. Verse 6.

When we were going through the second chakra of Creativity and Emotions, we saw that the mind is regarded as a separate element in itself. The reason being its infinite potential and the quality it has to disassociate itself with other sense organs and the physical world as is. As a salesperson your minds are constantly processing information. You plan. You prospect. You pitch. You negotiate. You close. You manage. There are so many tasks that make up the daily schedule for a salesperson. In all this chatter that the mind goes through hearing what your intuition is telling you becomes a huge challenge. Almost impossible to do. That is where

Dhyan Yoga is a method to reach this place so you can be friends with your mind and not make it your greatest enemy.

This is the opportunity you are giving yourself to open up your connection with yourself and through it to the world of customers and prospects around you. The one waiting to be converted in your CRM. Let me summarize the matter of intuition and the need to practice Dhyana Yoga and harness it with the following verse. The bonus chapter on Meditation and Yoga by our expert guest, Jenil Dholakia will take you through the practices you can bring into your daily schedule.

यत्रोपरमते चित्तं निरुद्धं योगसेवया।
यत्र चैवात्मनाऽऽत्मानं पश्यन्नात्मनि तुष्यति।।
सुखमात्यन्तिकं यत्तद्बुद्धिग्राह्यमतीन्द्रियम्।
वेत्ति यत्र न चैवायं स्थितश्चलति तत्त्वतः।।
यं लब्ध्वा चापरं लाभं मन्यते नाधिकं ततः।
यस्मिन्स्थितो न दुःखेन गुरुणापि विचाल्यते।।
तं विद्याद् दुःखसंयोगवियोगं योगसंज्ञितम्।
स निश्चयेन योक्तव्यो योगोऽनिर्विण्णचेतसा।।

In the stage of trance, one's mind is completely restrained from material mental activities by practice of yoga. This perfection is characterized by one's ability to see the self by the pure mind and to relish and rejoice in the self, In that joyous state, one is situated in boundless transcendental

happiness. realized through transcendental senses. established thus, one never departs from the truth, and upon gaining this he thinks there is no greater gain. Being situated in such a position, one is never shaken, even in the midst of greatest difficulty. This indeed is actual freedom from all miseries arising from material contact.

Chapter 6. Verses 20-23.

Am sure you can sense the tone of the book change in this chapter to more meta concepts. It is true. The Ajna is a chakra that is beyond the elements and the best way to master and invoke this is to keep an open mind and follow the practices prescribed in the Bhagwad Gita and other branches of Yoga as in the bonus chapter.

One of my all-time quotes is by Frank Zappa where he says and I quote - "The mind is like a parachute. It doesn't work if it's not open."

As a Happiness Coach and practitioner, I am very aware of the power of an open mind. When I have used these principles in my sales life, the effect has been huge as the mind then doesn't recognize limitations and boundaries. From a passion perspective we saw in the third chapter, how lighting the fire where it matters is important. Going beyond what you already know is a characteristic that will surely take you places as a salesperson.

From the business perspective, it opens up new geographies, new product lines. new offerings. new services and new customers. Modern day psychology gives open mindedness the importance of a value. Values are positive. As a salesperson being open minded means your ability to understand perspectives improves ten folds. It means you will be able to accept the other perspectives and possibilities. While you may still disagree with some, an open mind instills in you the willingness to see the other person's beliefs and opinions as equally legitimate.

REFLECTION TIME #12:

Think of an event in your work of your life where you opened yourself to a new experience and it turned out to be a great experience for you. Note down the positive emotions you feel as you think about that event.

____

____

____

____

____

____

____

Be open as being closed is not an option for you. Not in sales.

If you are closed you will be angry, will only speak but not listen and will carry the weight of feeling you are always right. That in tone itself sounds very detrimental.

BONUS #5:
The Sales Yogi Ajna Affirmation Statement:

I embrace the inner voice and am open to the new as I am self-assured.

- The Sales Yogi learns from self-realization.
- The Sales Yogi exercises his/her intuitive capabilities through the prescribed Yoga techniques.
- The Sales Yogi meditates and clears the fog of his/her thoughts.
- The Sales Yogi is never self-restricted. He/She is open to what comes their way.
- The Sales Yogi focuses within to listen to and seek guidance from his/her intuition.

When you hear yourself clearly your confidence and conviction go up. The chapter went beyond the elemental nature of sales and the salesperson. As we saw that the soul or the life force within is supreme and even the best of intellect bows down before it. When you surrender to this inner self, you will see magic happening. More people will join in on your journey and your network and your influence on them improves dramatically. This influence and the network you build as a salesperson is the seventh and the last chakra - The Sahasara or the Crown.

THE SAHASRARA OF SALES - NETWORK AND INFLUENCE

सर्वतः पाणिपादं तत्सर्वतोऽक्षिशिरोमुखम्।
सर्वतः श्रुतिमल्लोके सर्वमावृत्य तिष्ठति।।

With hands and feet everywhere, with eyes, heads and mouths everywhere, with ears everywhere, He exists in the worlds enveloping all.

Chapter 13. Verse 14.

It has been a great day for Shalini. She has reached 25000 followers on her favorite social media platform. As a sales person it gives her the confidence that she can now reach more people and influence them - thereby increasing her sales numbers. She hopes to surpass Sangeetha and win the best salesperson award.

Sangeetha on the other hand has around 5000 followers but is the sales champion of her company. She says her real network is the people she is in actual touch with. In the old-fashioned way of calls and emails. Conversations that are actually contributing to her image as a great partner to work with and leading her to the sales targets. She feels grateful to be able to have the true connection with many of her prospects and she carries that goodness into the conversations and her network.

She says people love doing business with people!

The real crown of a salesperson is the network he/she has. The number of people who are just a phone call away.

This chakra is your gateway to what lies beyond your immediate circle of influence. The crown chakra of Network and Influence. Like our physical network the power of this chakra is infinite and boundless. Hence this too is not associated with any element in Yoga. The Sahasrara is depicted with a thousand petal lotus - as it literally means.

The current scenario of work and how sales is being done further amplifies the reach and influence you may have because of the internet and social networks. However, those are just enablers and my intention to include this aspect as the seventh chakra is not to provide you with the tips to increase your social network presence. My intention here is to tell you what intrinsically is going to help you create such an influence that you can transform your social presence and also hopefully impact lives.

With that intention set, I would like you to answer the below question.

REFLECTION TIME #13:

Why do you think anyone will want to connect with you and know you more?

____

____

____

____

____

____

____

____

If you answered the above question with what you are selling and the solution you provide, please rewrite it again. The answer to the above question is important for you to look at in perspective of yourself as a person. What makes you who you are? Do not attach your identity to the product or service you speak of everyday. That is a part of you. That is your duty and your penance like we saw.

As we gradually move from the root chakra of Attitude to the crown chakra of Network and Influence, we are transcending. Look at it like a funnel - an image all of you can easily relate to being salespeople and business owners. As we have progressed in this journey of being a Sales Yogi, we have gradually increased our circle of influence from things that are very intrinsic to the more meta and larger scheme of things. A small illustration of the journey thus far.

As a salesperson looking to increase the network and influence one of the key values to imbibe is Gratitude. It is only from the seat of goodness that you can truly be influential. This value has been hailed by many as one of the most important values one has to imbibe to live a very peaceful and happy life. Gratitude is something that can be practiced every day and that is something I encourage participants in my Happiness Coaching initiatives to do.

So how can Gratitude actually help you increase your influence?

निर्मानमोहा जितसङ्गदोषा
अध्यात्मनित्या विनिवृत्तकामाः।
द्वन्द्वैर्विमुक्ताः सुखदुःखसंज्ञै
र्गच्छन्त्यमूढाः पदमव्ययं तत्।।

Those who are free from false prestige, illusion and false association, who understand the eternal, who are done with material lust, who are freed from the dualities of happiness and distress, and who, un-bewildered, know how to surrender, attain to that Eternal Kingdom.

Chapter 15. Verse 5.

The life of a salesperson is filled with action. Fast paced. Ruthless. In all this speed, it is important to enjoy the journey. Slowing down and embracing the need to relax is important like we saw in the last chapter. When we do this, we have time to truly appreciate and be thankful. Gratitude in essence means this. It is the quality of being thankful and the readiness to show appreciation for and return kindness. When you as a salesperson are seated in the position of gratitude, you will see that the efforts needed to connect with your prospects and customers is almost nil. People sense the genuine and good and they are naturally attracted to these vibes.

Let me share a few tips on how you can be a grateful salesperson and thereby increase your influence.

1. Be patient. Yes, I know this is a repetition. But please bear with me. Patience is the virtue that will help you especially when things are not going your way. No one likes to keep in contact with someone who exudes desperation and neediness. It stems from a selfish place and your customers are smart enough to sniff that out.

2. Share the success of your connections and customers. Be genuinely happy for them and share in their joys. Be there when you know they are going through a tough time. People remember how you made them feel.

With Gratitude you will be able to radiate goodness effortlessly.

3. Pay it forward. Any good deed or any favor you get from your network, pay it forward. Everything good exponentially increases as it is paid forward. Thank and count your blessings and strive to make every person you interact with feel the same.

4. It's all about the people! Sales is people's work. Building and nurturing relationships for a huge part of what you do. Practicing gratitude will help you stay focused on the human element of sales. I have highlighted how you as a salesperson have the power to create and change. When you enjoy that power why not use it to be a force of good in the world?

5. Welcome the downs with open arms like you will welcome the highs. Gratitude can help you navigate the ups and downs of life as a sales person. Gratitude helps in maintaining perspective and focusing on the larger goal even when you are having the worst day in your sales career!

6. Appreciation is almost always reciprocated. Your customers will rarely change their partners for a particular product or service due to cost or performance. Unless you seriously botch up the two, the chances are that look elsewhere because of lack of engagement. You have to make your

customers feel appreciated for their business. Let me warn you again. Say Thank You because you mean it and not because you have been told to say so.

You have understood how you can practice gratitude in sales too and how it will increase your influence on your network. Being good is one of the easiest things to do as it really does not need any thinking or motivation. So, go ahead and radiate that goodness to your network. To understand this in your individual context let's reflect.

REFLECTION TIME #14:

Think about an interaction with a client that you are truly grateful for. It need not be a positive event. It could be one deal you lost that taught you the most important lesson in sales. Write down why you are grateful for that interaction and what elements of it still make you feel thankful.

____

____

____

____

____

____

____

BONUS #7

Gratitude is something that is best felt when practiced daily. Sharing a framework of gratitude journal that has helped my coachees imbibe this value in them - even when things are not going their way. Use it daily. You will be amazed with the increase in the quality of interactions you have with your customers and colleagues.

Today at work I was grateful for these three things:

____

____

____

____

I am grateful to this one customer of mine today because:

____

____

____

____

Today was made special because:

____

____

____

____

This is one framework that will help you make a note of the good things every day. When you note these down you eventually realize how there is always something and someone to be grateful for in a day. Especially for a salesperson who interacts with people every day.

BONUS #8

The Sales Yogi Sahasrara Affirmation Statement:

I surrender to the goodness with which I truly influence my network and beyond.

- The Sales Yogi realizes true influence is the influence of doing good.
- The Sales Yogi embraces Gratitude as one his/her key qualities.
- The Sales Yogi fails fast and moves ahead in his/her duties.
- The Sales Yogi maintains a gratitude journal every day.
- The Sales Yogi pays the goodness forward.

As you increase your influence and further your repute as a person who puts the clients first and maintains your goodness, you attain the power to sustain your growth as a salesperson. Your network thus increases in the quality of interactions and not only in the quantity of connections. This brings us to the end of all the seven chakras.

Through the book we saw some useful verses from the Bhagwad Gita that enabled you to understand the nuance of each of the seven chakras of sales. Let's summarize the qualities of the one with divine nature - you, The Sales Yogi.

अभयं सत्त्वसंशुद्धिः ज्ञानयोगव्यवस्थितिः।
दानं दमश्च यज्ञश्च स्वाध्यायस्तप आर्जवम्।।
अहिंसा सत्यमक्रोधस्त्यागः शान्तिरपैशुनम्।
दया भूतेष्वलोलुप्त्वं मार्दवं ह्रीरचापलम्।।
तेजः क्षमा धृतिः शौचमद्रोहो नातिमानिता।
भवन्ति सम्पदं दैवीमभिजातस्य भारत।।

Fearlessness, purification of one's existence, cultivation of spiritual knowledge; charity; self-control; performance of sacrifice; study of the Vedas; austerity; simplicity; nonviolence; truthfulness; freedom from anger; renunciation; tranquility; aversion to faultfinding; compassion for all living entities; freedom from covetousness; gentleness; modesty; steady determination;vigor; forgiveness; fortitude; cleanliness; and freedom from envy and from the passion for honor - these transcendental qualities, O Son of Bharata, belong to godly men endowed with divine nature.

Chapter 16. Verses 1-3.

We saw how these are not just qualities that sound good but can be made a part of who you are and what you do. The Karma Yogi never digresses from the duties and moves ahead with utmost devotion and love for what he/she is doing.

Be all that and much more. Embrace the power within you. Blossom through its nourishment. Nourishment that you will give yourself with the seven chakras of sales.

Once again, Happy Selling my dear Yogis!

BONUS

CHAPTERS

In this bonus chapter we look at Yoga and Pranayama. Guiding us through this purpose of covering Yoga and Pranayama into the daily schedule of a Sales Yogi will be Jenil Dholakia.

Jenil comes with great knowledge and insights into the field of Yoga and Pranayama. Let's get straight into the chapter which is in an interview format of my conversation with Jenil.

Me: Tell our readers more about yourself and your story of how you started on this journey of healing through Yoga and Pranayama.

Jenil: My journey from a desk job to a yoga mat has been quite an experimental one. After spending nearly, a decade working in the events industry, I found yoga to heal my persistent problem of PCOD/ PCOS which was creating quite a havoc in my life, physically, emotionally & mentally. When all the conventional medicine routes did not help, I found solace in yoga. As I pursued it more, I discovered how much more there was to yoga then just its physical aspect. It got me hooked & I booked myself for an intensive teacher training program at Rishikesh. Then, there was simply no looking back. I said farewell to my job & embraced the path of yoga wholeheartedly. Today the corporate books have been replaced by philosophy books, the demanding clients by caring students, and the office chair by a yoga mat. It has not been an easy journey – and I am still making my way on it – but I would not have it any other way.

Yoga has provided me the tools to take what I have learnt on the mat which is strength, focus, flexibility, compassion & patience and to apply it in the world where it really counts.

I love travelling & decided to explore the riches of Yogic wisdom at various Ashrams in India - Rishukul Yogashala in Rishikesh; Swami Vivekananda Yoga Anusandhana Samsthana, [SVYASA], Bangalore; Kaivalyadham, Lonavala; The Yoga Institute, Mumbai; International Academy of Sound Healing [IASH], Calcutta; Vipassana Meditation Center, Igatpuri; Osho Ashram, Pune; only to provide the best to my students.

Currently, I have been teaching the authentic art of yoga across the globe for over 5 years now. I love bringing yoga into the lives of more & more people. Over the years of practicing the various schools of yoga - Hatha, Ashtanga, Vinyasa flow, Iyengar yoga, etc.; I culminate the essence of these different styles in my unique manner. On and off the mat, I wish to provide a space that encourages one to explore their inner being, discover the true self and unlock layers of past conditionings. My classes are filled with people of all ages, languages, and cultures - where all bodies are welcome and the common spirit is celebrated.

I want to give back to others what yoga has sparked in me. Through my teachings, I wish to continue sharing this love of yoga with the world, one breath at a time, one being at a time! I truly believe that yoga is a practice that meets you where you are and takes you where you want to go.

Lastly, I am grateful and honoured that this is what I get to do every single day of my life. Hoping that my path with the readers here will cross someday on a yoga mat!

Me: Why do you think it is important for people in the sales field to take care of their mind and body?

Jenil: Sales is hard work. It involves long working hours, demanding targets, tight deadlines, requires meticulous preparation, understanding customer needs and concerns, complete focus & clarity of thought. All of this can obviously take on the toll on your wellbeing in the long run & eventually make you less productive at work. That is why it is extremely important to regularly make time to de-stress, relax and re-energize.

While there are many methods to do that – Yoga is one of the most powerful and effective ways to work holistically on your body & mind together. If you take care of your mind & body, you will be better equipped to handle whatever challenges you have to face that day, your immunity will increase, you will create balance in your life, reduce anxiety, will help you sleep better, uplift your mood & ultimately help you achieve those sales targets successfully!

Me: As a salesperson, what morning routine of Yoga and Pranayama can one follow?

Jenil: It's very important to start your day on the right note as it sets the tone for the rest of the day. Here are a few things that you can adapt in your morning routine:

Wake Up & Get Going:

Immediately after waking up, while you are still on your bed, take a moment to wake up the whole body with some gentle stretches. Take a deep breath, stretch your hands up & get ready to face the day. Since the spine has been in the lying down position for the whole night, show some love to it by doing a simple forward bend [Child's Pose /Balasana] as you take a moment of gratitude.

Open the windows, get some fresh air, wash your face, have some warm water. If you wake up in time for sunrise, spend those few minutes enjoying the early morning sun and the healing rays.

Sit for some time in silent meditation. You can also do pranayama to help you focus your mind.

Here are 3 pranayama techniques that you can do daily:

Samavritti Pranayama [Equal Breathing]
The objective here is to equalize the length of your inhalation & exhalation by deep soft & long breathing. It starts to improve your breathing capacity & stabilizes your breath.

Anulom Viloma (Alternate Nostril Breathing)
It purifies the nadis, which are channels carrying the vital energy & balances both the sides of your nostrils. As you keep on alternating the breath from one nostril to another, it induces tranquility and helps to improve concentration.

Bhramari [Humming Bee Breath]
This is one of the best pranayama that relieves stress and helps in alleviating anxiety, anger and hyperactivity. The resonance effect of humming sound creates a soothing effect on the mind and calms the nervous system.

Make time for some physical practice & get some movement in the morning. Here are a few yoga asanas that you can practice in the morning:

Suksma Vyayamas [Gentle stretching]
They help in increasing microcirculation in the body.

Standing Postures

Tadasana [Palm Tree pose]
This asana brings stability in the body, helps to clear up congestion of the spinal nerves, and corrects faulty posture.

Vrikshasana (Tree Pose)
This asana improves neuro-muscular coordination, balance, endurance and alertness.

Pada-Hastasana (Hands to Feet Pose)
This asana makes the spine flexible, improves digestion, prevents constipation and creates a sense of surrender.

Sitting Postures

Bhadrasana (The Firm/ Auspicious Posture)
This asana keeps the body firm and helps to stabilize the mind.

Paschimottanasana (Seated Forward bend)
This asana removes the tightness in legs & massages all the abdominal organs.

Vakrasana (Spinal Twisting)
This asana helps to increases flexibility of the spine & overcomes constipation.

Prone Postures

Bhujangasana (Cobra Pose)
This asana releases backache and expands the chest for better breathing.

Salabhasana (Locust Poste)
This asana massages the abdominal organs aiding digestion & gives a deep stretch to the spine.

Makarasana (Crocodile Pose)
This asana helps in recovery of back problems & counters stress and anxiety

Supine Postures

Setubandhasana (Bridge Pose)
This asana stretches abdominal organs and strengthens lower back muscles.

Pavanmuktasana (Wind Releasing Pose)
This asana decreases the bloating sensation in the abdomen and aids digestion.

Savasana (Corpse Pose)
This asana helps to relieve all kinds of tensions and gives rest to both body and mind.

I hope all of you have gained some amount of clarity in terms of the Yoga and Pranayama practices that will help you deal with the stress of sales better. We have not given details on every pose and how to do them here as the idea of the chapter was to provide you with the exact methods you can start doing from the expert's perspective. If you wish to learn these in detail, feel free to reach out to Jenil Dholakia. Her contact details are given below.

Email: jenildholakia.yoga@gmail.com
Instagram: @jenildholakia.yoga
Facebook Page: Jenil Dholakia Yoga
Website: www.jenildholakiayoga.com

I am sure the last chapter would have given you some useful and handy tips.

But the journey does not stop here. As a salesperson, I am very aware of how much one ignores food and diet when on duty. Like good fuel is important to keep the vehicle running, good food is necessary to sustain one's energy level and overall wellbeing. After all, it is said that every illness starts from the gut.

To guide us through this aspect we have Mugdha Pradhan - a leading functional nutritionist. Here is my interview with her on this important aspect of food and what salespeople can do to ensure health.

Me: Tell our readers more about yourself and your story of how you started on this journey of healing through food.

Mugdha: I have a Master's degree in Nutrition and have spent close to two decades in the arena of health and wellness. I discovered Functional Medicine when my own health took a nosedive. Using modern principles of functional medicine along with ancient wisdom about food and basing it on a sound foundation of spirituality I recovered from a multitude of chronic illnesses- not only did I lose 37 kgs, but I also reversed an autoimmune thyroid dysfunction (Hashimotos), diabetes and depression. I founded Thrive in 2017 to help others heal from chronic illnesses with my simple systems and methods. I have successfully healed over 200 unique cases so far. I have the vision of healing 1 Million people through ThriveFNC.

Me: Why do you think it is important for people in the sales field to take care of what they eat?

Mugdha: Being on the field is quite physically demanding and can drain energy even from the best of us. Besides which anyone in the sales role really has to maintain higher energy levels all the time, because if they are low on energy internally- leads and prospects sense it and will not want to buy whatever it is you are selling. For these two precise reasons, a lot of field sales people become dependent on stimulants like tea/ coffee and cigarettes just so that they have the energy they need to get through the day.

This is where food becomes really important, even if someone is on the field for long hours, if they take care of supplying their body with nutrient dense foods and hydrating themselves frequently, they WILL be exhaustion free. The right kind of food can fuel the body with limitless energy, while the wrong kind of food (typical street food or conveniently available junk food) can deplete your body of energy and result in sluggishness, fatigue and lethargy.

Me: From the overall wellbeing perspective, The Bhagwad Gita too recommends eating the right food. What is your opinion on the contribution food makes to the overall wellbeing?

Mugdha: Food is the most powerful medicine on this planet. Food is not just calories. We literally use food for everything other than what it is. We use food as entertainment, we use food as a boredom fixer, we use food as our emotional back-up system, we use food as a social networking system. But food is none of that. Food is information. It's actual instructions, like a code that can be used to upgrade or downgrade your biological software. You can change your genes by what you put in your mouth. Every bite you take can either upgrade your genes or downgrade them. Every bite you take can trigger your genes into expressing either health or disease.

I firmly believe food has a big, big role to play in the overall well-being of a human being and I agree with the Bhagwad Gita here.

Me: As a salesperson, what dietary precautions should one take?

Mugdha: Again, going back to previous question, the focus should be on eating nutrient dense foods (aka foods that give a lot of nutrition even in the smallest quantity) so that you fulfill your body's needs without feeling heavy or bloated and on avoiding foods that are filled with empty calories (such as sugar, refined oils, processed foods)

But even before going to dietary precautions, I'd actually recommend getting your internal health checked. A lot of people go through life without realizing their tiredness, fatigue, headaches etc. could all be indicative of underlying deficiencies of Iron, B-12, or Vitamin D. Sometimes conditions such as insulin resistance prevents your body from creating and utilizing energy when you need it most resulting in tiredness.

So, before you start thinking about what to eat, learn what's your internal state like and what are the corrective actions you need to take to ensure everything is working well internally. What you should eat becomes an automatic outcome of this.

Me: With the running around and erratic schedules, what tips can you provide regarding food that will help the salesperson stay away from junk food?

Mugdha:

1. Hydrate well and often- a lot of people mistake thirst for hunger and end up eating quick, convenient junk food to quench that feeling of thirst-hunger

2. Carry boiled eggs, dates, roasted chana, fruits or homemade healthy cookies (recipe here) as healthy snack items

3. If you are willing to experiment with nutritional ketosis, it's ideal for someone with erratic schedules as the body is in a steady energy producing- fat burning state and one generally doesn't experience cravings and random hunger pangs. You can go for long periods without the need to eat and still not feel exhausted. It's my personal favorite way to be when I have long days or lots of travel in my schedule.

4. Lastly, don't eat food like a chore. Enjoy and relish your food when you eat it, after all every bite you eat is going to become part of your body. If you choose wisely then you are going to be creating an incredibly healthy, resilient and strong body.

Food is an important aspect and one should not ignore it. Mugdha can guide you more in this regard and if you are keen to get your personal profiling done, please do get in touch with her through the email ID below:

hello@thrivefnc.com

CONCLUSION

We have come to the end of this journey of being a Yogi in Sales.

The book and its contents are aimed at making sales life easier and success surer. But these are concepts that are valid for every person who is working or following their dreams.

Everything we know stems from our attitude towards it. It is therefore the Mooladhara for everything you will do in life. To focus on that is to ensure that the journey ahead is much more fruitful.

As you went through this book, you have seen me tell you numerous times to keep an open mind and look at your work as your duty and not a task. The small shift in mindset may not seem very impactful, but it made Arjuna the most celebrated warrior. Be a karma yogi in the true sense of it. Am summarizing the chapters in this book here with the affirmation statements. Write them down again and paste it up on your work desk.

The Sales Yogi Attitude
- Mooladhara Chakra Affirmation Statement:

I am grounded and I know I am a channel. I do not do things, I make things happen AS me.

Summarizing the traits that make up for the Attitude or the Mooladhara Chakra of a Sales Yogi:

- The Sales Yogi is dutiful.
- The Sales Yogi understands that he/she is meant to sell and focuses on the larger vision at hand.
- The Sales Yogi knows how action and inaction are all part of the duty and sets his/her attention to mastering these and being a true *Karma Yogi*.
- The Sales Yogi is attached to action and not the fruits of the action.
- The Sales Yogi is humble and grounded.
- The Sales Yogi embraces his/her role in the organization and understands that he/she is the chosen channel for the success of the organization, no matter where they are in the hierarchy.

The Sales Yogi Creativity & Emotions
- Swadhisthana Chakra Affirmation Statement:

I create great opportunities. I am a master of what and how I feel.

Summarizing some important elements that make up for mastering the Chakra of Creativity and Emotions for a Sales Yogi:

- The Sales Yogi enjoys the state of flow stemming from the attitude.
- Like water, the Sales Yogi is fluid and adaptable. Free in thoughts and emotions, the Sales Yogi is not bound or controlled by either.
- The Sales Yogi has the potential to create or shape his/her reality.
- The Sales Yogi strives to understand the emotions that operate in the field of activity and control his/her reaction to them.
- The Sales Yogi is firm and courageous in the face of distress or anger as he/she knows that is what will sustain.

The Sales Yogi Passion, Persistence & Knowledge
– Manipura Chakra Affirmation Statement:

I am powerful and steadfast. My light shines through my knowledge of myself and beyond.

- The Sales Yogi knows his three jewels are his passion, persistence, and knowledge.

- The Sales Yogi realizes channelizing passion is important as it has the quality to burn like fire.
- The Sales Yogi understands that everything that makes him/her persistent is always something he/she can control.
- The Sales Yogi knows that knowledge of academia is just half knowledge. True power comes from self-realization.
- The Sales Yogi concentrates on certain qualities that are important and strives to increase his/her knowledge on these aspects to empower themselves.

The Sales Yogi Client Centricity
– Anahata Chakra Affirmation Statement:

I am the seat of goodness for my customers. Through me, they grow and change.

- The Sales Yogi is devoted to his customer.
- The Sales Yogi builds and nurtures relationships.
- The Sales Yogi understands the concept of Bhakti Yoga and strives to practice it every day.
- The Sales Yogi knows he/she holds the power within to impact and do good.
- The Sales Yogi Imbibes the five key qualities that will lead him to be a preferred partner to his/her clients.

The Sales Yogi Communication & Expression
– Vishuddha Chakra Affirmation Statement:

I speak to be authentic. I listen to inspire change.

- The Sales Yogi is truthful and authentic in speech.
- The Sales Yogi strives to be courteous and puts the interest of the other person ahead in a conversation.
- The Sales Yogi looks to constantly improve the art of effective communication through practice and observation.
- The Sales Yogi understands that fine speech is as much a gift as it is a penance.
- The Sales Yogi listened intently and without cavil.
- The Sales Yogi identifies the personal and emotional barriers and puts them aside to make communication mutually beneficial.

The Sales Yogi Intuition & Openness
- Ajna Affirmation Statement:

I embrace the inner voice and am open to the new as I am self-assured.

- The Sales Yogi learns from self-realization.
- The Sales Yogi exercises his/her intuitive capabilities through the prescribed Yoga techniques.
- The Sales Yogi meditates and clears the fog of his/her thoughts.

- The Sales Yogi is never self-restricted. He/ She is open to what comes their way.
- The Sales Yogi focuses within to listen to and seek guidance from his/her intuition.

The Sales Yogi Network & Influence
– Sahasrara Chakra Affirmation Statement:

I surrender to the goodness with which I truly influence my network and beyond.

- The Sales Yogi realizes true influence is the influence of doing good.
- The Sales Yogi embraces Gratitude as one his/her key qualities.
- The Sales Yogi fails fast and moves ahead in his/her duties.
- The Sales Yogi maintains a gratitude journal every day.
- The Sales Yogi pays the goodness forward.

The final verse of the 18th Chapter of the Bhagwad Gita says –

यत्र योगेश्वरः कृष्णो यत्र पार्थो धनुर्धरः।
तत्र श्रीर्विजयो भूतिर्ध्रुवा नीतिर्मतिर्मम।।

Where there is Krsna, the Lord of the Yogas, and where there is Partha, the wielder of the bow, there are fortune, victory, prosperity and unfailing prudence. Such is my conviction.

The amazing concepts of Karma Yoga, Bhakti Yoga, Dhyan Yoga and many others mentioned in this book are your guiding force. I urge each and every one who reads this book to imbibe these as Arjuna did.

The more you practice these the more surer your chances of being a star salesperson, with fortune, victory, prosperity, and unfailing prudence defining who you are!

That is my conviction for you, like Sanjaya's words in the above verse.

THANK YOU

Thank You For Reading My Book!

I really appreciate all of your feedback, and I love hearing what you have to say.

I need your input to make the next version of this book and my future books even better.

Please leave me a helpful review on Amazon letting me know what you thought of the book.

I also run sales coaching journeys for individuals and teams. For more information head on to
www.thesalesyogi.me

As a token of appreciation for your patronage, please use the code BOOK25 at checkout to aval 25% discount on the flagship Seven Chakras of Sales Program.

Other links to keep in touch:

Podcast: www.salesyogipodcast.com

LinkedIn: **linkedin.com/in/sanjeevvksomanath**

Thank you so much!
Sanjeevv K Somanath

REFERENCES

The Bhagwad Gita As It is by His Divine Grace A C Bhaktivedanta Swami Prabhupada

https://yogainternational.com/article/view/ what-are-the-7-chakras